SUNKEN EGYPT

ALEXANDRIA

Published by Periplus Publishing London Ltd, 2004
Publisher: Danièle Juncqua Naveau
Managing editor: Nick Easterbrook
Assistant editor: Jenny Finch
Production manager: Sophie Chéry
Editorial collaboration: Raphaële Vidaling
Translation from the French: Ruth Sharman

© 2004, Periplus Publishing London Ltd, The Sorting Office, 21 Station Road, London, SW13 0LF, UK
Printed and bound in Italy by Graphicom

ISBN : 1-902699-51-3

SUNKEN EGYPT

ALEXANDRIA

FRANCK GODDIO

ANDRÉ BERNAND

Periplus

London

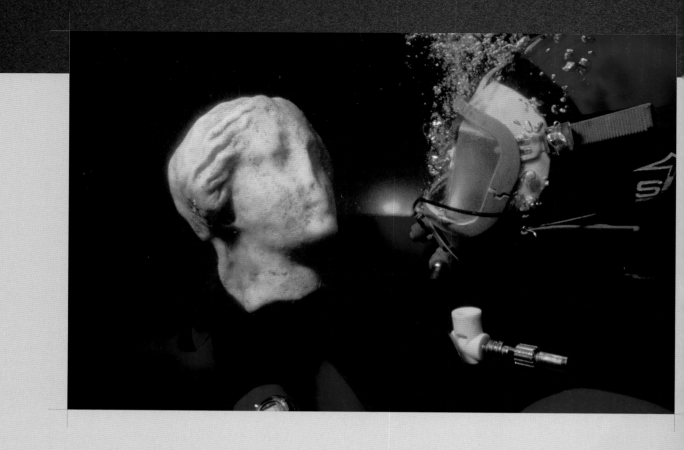

CONTENTS

A figure representing the city of Alexandria appears on a mosaic discovered at Thmouis, a town in the Egyptian delta. The mosaic is the work of a certain Sophilos and shows Alexandria personified as a woman wearing a ship's prow on her head and holding a mast and a yard.

This figure is almost certainly meant to be regarded as the 'wife' of Alexander the Great, who metaphorically speaking married his destiny.

It is probably closer to the mark, in fact, to think of Alexandria as Alexander himself – an extraordinary man who conferred his own exceptional gifts on the city that bore his name.

A soldier turned town planner

Nothing predisposed Alexander the Great to found a city. The general was only 25 years old when he traced the outlines of Alexandria, with the assistance of the architect Deinocrates of Rhodes and the army engineers Diades and Kharias. He chose the grid layout recommended by the architect Hippodamus of Miletus, a contemporary of Pericles, and drew the shape of the city in flour to resemble a soldier's tunic, or *chlamys*. The plan was executed on 20 January 331 BC, the 25th day of the Egyptian month of Tybi.

Up until this date, Alexander's experience of life had been uniquely bound up with war. At the age of 16, he had already acted as quasi-regent, exercising power in the absence of his father Philip II of Macedonia and taking responsibility for the royal seal. Even at that time he may have been debating ways of organising and extending his father's kingdom (we will see why in due course). In any event, he was used to the upheavals of endless military campaigns, and used to holding a position of command. In 338 BC, he took part in the battle of Chaeronea in Boeotia, where his father defeated the joint forces of the Athenians and the Thebans, thereby ensuring Macedonian supremacy. In the years that followed, Alexander engaged in a list of campaigns long enough to rival Napoleon's. In October 332 BC, he took Pelusium, the key to Egypt, and in December of the same year he received the title of Pharaoh at Memphis. He then removed his army to the western delta.

Alexander's battles were the stuff of epics. His courage and determination became legendary and are written all over his face in the Casa del Fauno mosaic, at Pompeii, which shows him pursuing Darius III of Persia on his famous horse Bucephalus.

Like those other great cities of the Mediterranean world, Athens, Rome and Byzantium, Alexandria embodied a unique civilisation: just as we can speak of Athenian and Byzantine civilisation, so we can speak of Alexandrian civilisation. These generic terms encompass complex realities, however, particularly in the case of Alexandria, which combined the inheritance of Egyptian and also of Roman and Christian civilisation.

A city in the image of its founder

Alexandria reflected the character traits of its founder, above all his courage and self-possession – qualities that Alexander demonstrated at a young age by taming the fiery horse Bucephalus, which no one else had succeeded in mounting. Observing that the creature was frightened by its own shadow, Alexander realised that all he had to do to calm the horse was to face it into the sun. And when it came to building his city, Alexander designed it, likewise, facing the sea, which constituted a permanent threat (as will become clear in relation to its coasts and harbours). The young general understood that, in order to survive and flourish, the new city had to obey three imperatives: it had to be able to defend itself against potential invaders, it had to be able to feed itself, and it had to be able to grow. The sea and the deserts were natural defences; the delta and the rest of Egypt provided a fertile *chora*, a territory of inexhaustible riches; and, finally, the city could extend towards the borders with Libya in the west and the Aboukir plain and the wide expanses of the delta in the east. Fresh water, meanwhile (which could otherwise have posed an insoluble problem), was supplied by the canal known, appropriately enough, as the 'good spirit' and which connected the river harbour and the Nile, like an umbilical cord feeding the nascent city.

Alexander recognised the difficulties, and the advantages, of the terrain. All he had to do to turn the hinterland into a swamp impassable to either men or horses, was demolish the earth embankments holding back the water in the irrigation canals. In the 3rd century AD, Achilles Tatius described a skirmish between the Alexandrians and the wild, warlike inhabitants of the delta: *it was an unprecedented disaster: so many shipwrecks and not a single ship! Two things were extraordinary, contrary to all expectations: an infantry engagement in the water, and a shipwreck on land!* Vivant Denon and his companions found themselves in similar circumstances during Napoleon's Egyptian campaign, and the episode clearly illustrates the dangers that awaited Alexander…

André Bernand

An atypical career path

Grandson of the navigator Éric de Bisschop – a sailor, writer and expert on ancient sea routes in the South Pacific – Franck Goddio has two passions in life: history and the sea. At the age of 37, at the height of a brilliant career, he abandoned his suit and tie and devoted his energies to a new, and highly successful, vocation as an underwater archaeologist.

Franck Goddio, director of the Institut européen d'archéologie sous-marine (IEASM).

Born in Casablanca, of an Italian father and a Breton mother, Franck Goddio is one of those people who feel at home anywhere in the world, and particularly in the no-man's-land that belongs to all of us and none of us – the sea. As a child, he was already dreaming about archaeology. He went on excavations organised for young people, dragged his parents to one museum and ancient site after another, and read every history book he could lay his hands on. Following a scientific training, he worked for 12 years in the world of economics and finance, which gave him the opportunity to travel – mainly in Asia, the Middle East and Africa – and also to develop a rigorous, analytical approach which was to serve him so well when he switched disciplines and became an archaeologist. The same skills would be required of him: the same bias towards minute examination and exhaustive list-making, the same scientific mentality.

After careful thought, Franck decided to give up a career that was by now firmly launched and indulge his passions for sailing and historical research. Underwater archaeology (at the time still a relatively young discipline) shared common ground with both these interests and seemed the ideal answer.

An early mentor

Career changes are often prompted by an external agent playing the role of an initiator. Franck owed his initiation – and his first steps underwater – to Jacques Dumas, who also became an archaeologist after having pursued a career in another field (that of law). As president of the Fédération mondiale de plongée sous-marine (World Scuba Diving Federation), Jacques had undertaken to excavate the *Orient*, Napoleon's flagship, which was sunk by Nelson in 1798 in Aboukir Bay. He told Franck the history of the site – how it had taken six years of persistent effort, researching the archives, battling with all manner of red tape, and assembling the necessary manpower and materials, to reach this point of readiness – and then invited him to join him on the project for his first dive on an underwater excavation. Franck still speaks of the experience with emotion. "At a depth of 12m, the remains of the ship were gigantic," he recounts. "The rudder, 11m long, had become detached. Jacques was running out of air and I was on my own, facing the monster. I thought I could see something on one of the bronze reinforcements. I cleaned the area and an inscription appeared: 'Dauphin Royal'. So Jacques was wrong! Back up on deck, I asked him: 'Are you absolutely sure that this is the *Orient*?' With some considerable embarrassment, I told him about my discovery and, to my great surprise, he jumped for joy: 'Terrific! That's further confirmation: according to my research, *Dauphin Royal* was the name of the *Orient* before the Revolution! Well done, mon vieux. You seem to be cut out for diving…'"

It was a stroke of pure luck, but Franck took it to heart.

In 1985, he founded the Institut europeén d'archéologie sous-marine (IEASM) or European Institute of Underwater Archaeology, an organisation whose aim was to identify underwater archaeological sites, excavate and study them, and finally restore the recovered artefacts and display them to the public. Franck knew that he would have to fund the research himself, but he hoped that, if he could come up with some convincing results, he would eventually be able to persuade somebody to back him. He still had to prove himself as an archaeologist. He gave himself five years: it was to take seven.

Starting from scratch

Following the Aboukir episode, Franck contacted the Egyptian authorities, who were enthusiastic about the possibility of underwater research. A gigantic puzzle involving various civilisations lay scattered off the coasts of Egypt, the vital pieces hidden somewhere at the bottom of the sea; but as yet there were no detection instruments sufficiently sensitive to tackle the ambitious task of recovering them. Franck vowed, however, that one day he would come back to explore this fabulous terrain.

He assembled a team of specialists and together they took on a British East India Company vessel, the *Royal Captain*, sunk in the China Sea, in the Philippines. In the course of these excavations, they were astonished to discover pieces of Ming china that pre-dated the ship itself by two centuries. It turned out that the china had come from a 16th-century Chinese junk which had sunk close to the English vessel and was covered in coral. So, here was a second stroke of luck…

Franck turned his attentions next to the *Griffin*, another English vessel, sunk in the southern Philippines. Once again, the team carried out successful surveys of the area, but Franck was dissatisfied with their search techniques. What they needed, he decided, were more efficient magnetometers, since those that were available were neither reliable nor precise; but where were they to find them?

In 1988, he made contact with the team specialising in nuclear magnetic resonance at the Commission d'Energie Atomique (CEA), the French atomic energy commission. Its engineers had perfected magnetometric instruments whose sensitivity was a thousand times greater than that of their competitors. They regarded it as a challenge when Franck proposed that they adapt their material for use in the field of underwater archaeology. The two sides struck a bargain: Franck would put up some of the money for the research, and in exchange the Goddio team would be able to utilise the most sophisticated magnetometers in the world and benefit from the know-how of specialist engineers.

In 1992, at the end of seven years, Franck had excavated seven wrecks, published his findings and organised exhibitions of the archaeological material he had recovered, in particular a large number of Chinese ceramics dating from the 11th to the 18th centuries. He headed a tight-knit and highly competent multi-disciplinary team, supported by a network of leading scientists. A new generation of magnetometers was born and the IEASM owned exclusive world-wide rights to their use in archaeological applications. Franck now felt ready to contemplate returning to Egypt and pursuing his dream: to uncover the remains lying off the coast of Egypt, in the bays of Alexandria and Aboukir. His efforts would soon be rewarded by the discovery of the submerged Ptolemaic royal quarters.

The publisher

PART ONE

Underwater archaeology

What is underwater archaeology?

Underwater archaeology is a branch of general archaeology.
Both are employed in the service of history and share the same aims and principles.
What distinguishes them are the methods they use and their field of application.

Underwater archaeology employs the techniques of terrestrial archaeology in combination with skills specifically adapted to the aquatic environment. While confronting the destruction or burial of archaeological evidence by natural or human agents, it must also address the difficulties posed by diving. Because of the risks of decompression sickness it is not possible to spend protracted periods in deep water. Safety regulations only allow a diver to remain submerged at a depth of 30m for 15 minutes if he wishes to return to the surface without stopping for decompression. If he remains submerged for an hour, he is obliged to wait for 15 minutes when he rises to a depth of 6m, then a further 30 minutes at 3m. The length of time that the diver-archaeologist can spend underwater is therefore very limited. Furthermore, archaeological remains are frequently covered with a very thick layer – many tens of centimetres – of limestone deposits, or may be buried under several metres of sand, and to complete a mission of underwater excavations involves thousands of diving hours.

Reduced visibility is the other great difficulty faced by underwater archaeologists. Visibility may reach 30m in the Mediterranean in exceptional circumstances, but more often than not it is limited to 15 or 20m – and in the Bay of Alexandria, on really overcast days, this figure can be divided by 10 or 20.

Patience and care

Since artefacts have to be extracted from a site in order to be examined (even if they are later returned), excavations are inevitably disruptive. As operations proceed, it is therefore essential that all the data should be carefully recorded using modern techniques – and traditional ones too. There is no substitute, in fact, for the precise manual record which can be produced by a specialised draughtsman. Such a person is responsible for recording the conditions under which an object is found and will examine every element of a wreck, spending weeks underwater measuring the precise location and positioning of every object. Collecting various types of sample, studying the remains of a ship's hull, taking readings of the relative positions of different artefacts – all of this requires an uncommon degree of patience and care.

And yet the hours spent bogged down in mud, beleaguered by doubts and uncertainty, are not wasted, for those objects that are finally brought to light, and cleaned, analysed and identified, provide a precious contribution to our knowledge of the past. They serve as a guide, illuminating even the murkiest ocean bed. There is often a kind of magic at work here: the object that has been unearthed may suddenly give concrete reality to a past which previously seemed closer to a world of myth or dreams. Certainly, written texts provide us with information about the life of lost civilisations. However, nothing can equal the thrill of touching a sculpture which someone else – the sculptor – lovingly handled 2,000 years earlier, or following in the footsteps of Julius Caesar by walking (albeit with the palms of one's hands) on the stones once trodden by the emperor himself. Exhibited in museums thanks to the work of archaeologists, objects that have travelled through time give the public – or at least those prepared to use a little imagination – a real sense of human life as it was once lived.

Ceramic artefacts, like these, are the easiest to date with precision and can often be used as a guide to dating an entire site.

Fascinating wrecks

Wrecks are the favoured sites for archaeological excavations, generating intense interest on a number of counts. They may, for one thing, reveal valuable cargoes, works of art which have been better preserved by the sea than they would have been if exposed to various hazards on land. It was the search for such precious freight, in fact, which motivated the first underwater expeditions.

Wrecks are also the central focus of naval archaeology, a discipline in its own right, which specialises in the study of ship construction and technology. It is

A diver's first task consists of cleaning off deposits and then taking measurements. Only then can any attempt be made to identify the find – in this case a colossal head belonging to a statue of Caesarion, Cleopatra's son and the last of the Ptolemies.

A remarkable statue of a priest of Isis being raised to the surface. It has been cleaned of sediments and will now be handed over to the experts for examination. Found at Antirhodos, in Alexandria's eastern harbour.

The priest of Isis emerging into the sunlight after its 2,000 year sojourn on the seabed.

worth noting in passing that deposits forming around certain objects underwater can actually operate in our favour. Deposits that collect around iron preserve the object's shape when the iron disintegrates, thus furnishing us with precious information about materials in use at the time when it was produced.

Finally, over and above the material value of items which may be unearthed, shipwrecks provide us with a range of information regarding trade routes, the nature of goods exchanged, international relations, life on board ship, and naval warfare. A whole cross-section of civilisation may be brought to light.

A further reason for the scientific interest in wrecks – and one to which the public will invariably be sympathetic, as reactions to the *Titanic* demonstrate – lies in unravelling the mystery presented by such episodes in history, since every shipwreck conceals a drama, the causes of which frequently remain obscure. Archaeologists generally begin with a study of contemporary records, like detectives sifting through eye-witness accounts.

Time capsules

The excavation of a wreck clearly illustrates a major difference between terrestrial and underwater archaeology. If we were to start digging beneath the modern city of Alexandria, we would uncover the remains of the city built in the 1920s, then further down, evidence of mediaeval dwellings, remains from antiquity and, finally, when we reached the phreatic (groundwater) level, vestiges of the Ptolemaic era, drowned in an ocean of mud. The aim of terrestrial excavations is to uncover these successive and more or less distinct strata. Underwater explorations, on the other hand, can sometimes grant us access to a microcosm of society which has lain undisturbed for centuries – like a time capsule which we can touch with our fingertips.

Wreck sites provide the best example of this, since they tend to comprise artefacts from the same period and so furnish us with uniquely reliable indices for dating. Commercial cargoes are generally made up of goods whose manufacture is contemporary with that of the ship, so enabling us to establish close chronological groupings. Certain objects which, out of context, would be difficult to place in time can be dated fairly precisely since they occur together with others that are easy to date, such as coins. This characteristic of submerged sites is useful, for example, in the study of ceramics. Underwater archaeology contributes in this way to the establishment of a reliable chronology for little-known objects or items manufactured over a protracted period of time. It has aided the study of the remains of junks trading between China and the countries of southern Asia and has also focused attention on the Manila galleons and the ships of the East India Company, which later took over the local trade, sailing the ocean routes between Asia and the West.

Submerged worlds

Compared with the excavation of entire submerged sites, the excavation of a wreck appears little more than a simple training exercise, occurring within a specific area and focusing on a precise object. Attempting to retrace the contours of a drowned city is a task of quite a different magnitude, involving the archaeologist in a search for something whose nature and limits are unknown. A large part of the work consists therefore of determining the topography of the terrain. A geophysical approach identifies the sectors likely to conceal buildings or similar structures, and consequently the priority areas for intervention. And yet, despite the whole technological framework, intuition still plays a large part in the process: an area may be selected simply by chance, out of a number of alternatives, and exploration is often little better than fumbling in the dark.

A scientific approach does not exclude emotion; on the contrary, emotions are a natural concomitant of the quest for knowledge. Some of the objects recovered are pure works of art, and it is an extraordinary privilege to be able to admire them at leisure and so pay homage to the artists who created them. Others are modest, utilitarian objects, fragile messengers from the past which may, nevertheless, tell us a great deal about different areas of human interest.

Each day on board the support ship brings its harvest of information, and the boat is gradually transformed into a floating museum, a ship of dreams, laden with objects from another age. Preliminary measures are taken as soon as the artefacts reach the surface to ensure their conservation. There then begins a lengthy procedure involving further conservation, restoration, recording and systematic analysis. The results of this work are published in scientific journals and made accessible to the public through exhibitions, films and books.

Diver using an underwater suction device known as a water dredge to remove sediment accumulated over the course of two millennia.

Diver using a water dredge. Great care is needed: given the poor visibility, it would be easy to suck up a tiny artefact without noticing.

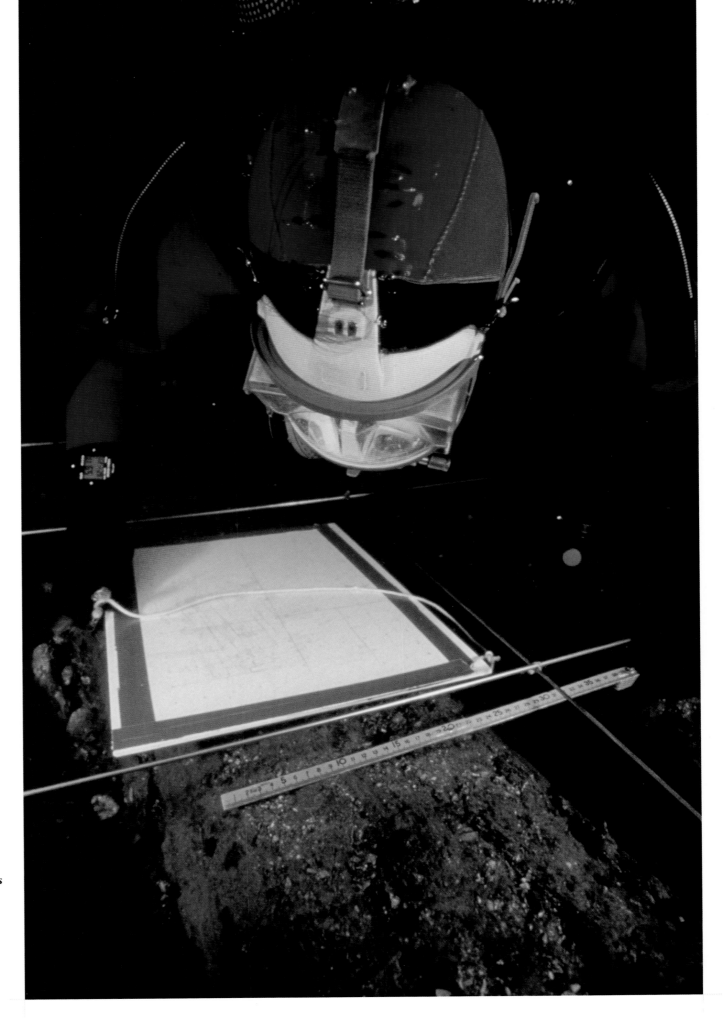

Many of the tools used in archaeology – here a measuring tape, slate and pencil – are the same whether the archaeologist is working underwater or on land. Artefacts are systematically measured and drawn before being recorded on the general excavation plan.

Objective: to draw a map of Alexandria

We were not the first people to want to explore the great capital of Ptolemaic Egypt. Numerous maps had already been drawn, though they were for the most part interpretations of classical texts, themselves only loosely based on reality. Our method was to examine all these documents, and then to put them to one side provisionally.

There is a long tradition of excavations at Alexandria. Many travellers and historians have dedicated their efforts to drawing up the plans of ancient Alexandria, often in somewhat empirical fashion. Here is an incomplete list of dates, authors and publications:

- 'Aegyptus Antiqua', by Abraham Ortelius, completed in 1570, published at Anvers in 1603 in *Theatrum orbis terrarum*;
- 'Plan d'Alexandrie' (inset: Alexandria), by M. D'Anville, in *Mémoires sur l'Egypte ancienne et moderne*, Paris, 1776;
- 'Plan of Alexandria', by Sir Gardner Wilkinson, London, 1843;
- 'Carte de l'antique Alexandrie et de ses faubourgs', by Mahmoud Bey El-Falaky, completed in 1866 and published in Copenhagen in 1872;
- 'Carte de l'ancienne Alexandrie', by Neroutsos Bey, Paris, 1866;
- 'Plan comparatif du port oriental d'Alexandrie sous les Ptolémées et à l'époque actuelle', by H. de Vaujany, Paris, 1888;
- 'Carte de l'ancienne Alexandrie', by G. Botti, 1898;
- 'Karten des alten Alexandria', by Wilhelm Sieglin, Leipzig, 1907;
- 'Alexandrie, plan de la ville ancienne et moderne', by E. Breccia, in *Alexandrea ad Aegyptum*, Bergamo, 1914.

Map of ancient Alexandria, drawn by Mahmoud Bey El-Falaky in 1866. The locations of the island of Antirhodos and the peninsula leading to the Timonium are reversed on this map.

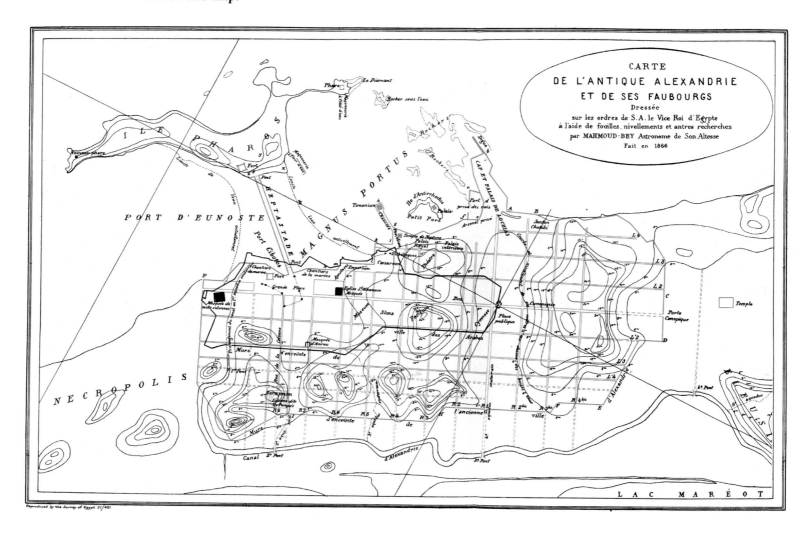

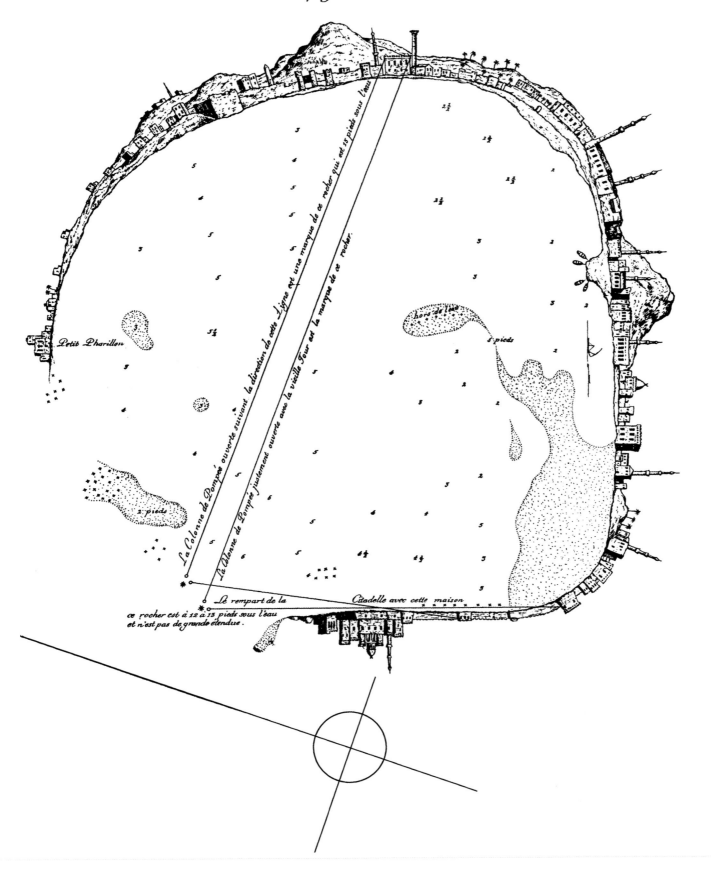

1738: map and plan of Alexandria's new harbour. Taken from Frederick Lewis Norden, Travels in Egypt and Nubia, Lockyer Davis & Charles Reymers, Holborn, Printers of the Royal Society, London, 1757.

Beginning in the second half of the 19th century, more detailed studies were to follow the accounts of 18th-century travellers and scholars. In 1865, Napoleon III decided to devote a book to Caesar's Alexandrian campaign. An engineer and astronomer by the name of Mahmoud El-Falaky, who was later elevated to the title of 'bey', and subsequently that of 'pasha', set about producing a map based as closely as possible on the supposed geography of the site in ancient times. Having mapped out a plan of the most recent Arab walls, which disappeared in 1882, he searched for the walls of the Greek city and found vestiges of these, too. By drilling boreholes he was able to confirm the assertions of ancient historians that the Roman streets intersected one another at right angles, in chequerboard fashion. El-Falaky collected and studied all the ancient texts, basing on these historical sources his suppositions regarding anything he was unable to verify on the ground. The maps that followed were largely inspired by El-Falaky's plan, but such reconstructions, based on physical remains, related to the terrestrial city: where the submerged part of the city was concerned there were no more than hypotheses to go on.

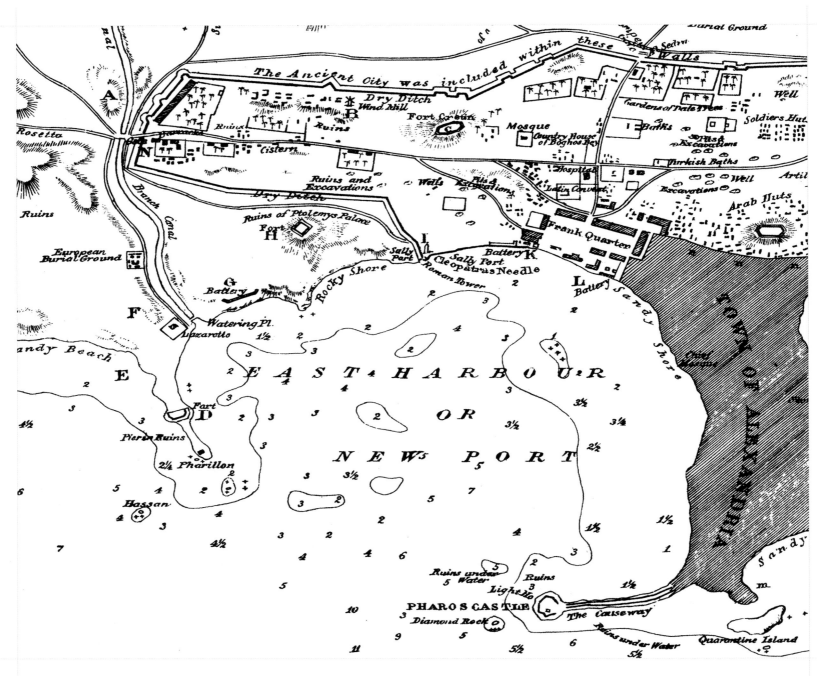

Plan of Alexandria and the surrounding area, 1841, by Lieutenant-Colonel E. Napier. Published by James Wyld, London, 1842.

Suspicions raised

A century later, in 1961, an amateur diver discovered the remains of a colossal statue near the Qait-Bey fort and eventually succeeded in persuading the Navy to raise it out of the water. The discovery of this monumental statue – the figure of a queen which must once have measured 13m – aroused the interest of the government and in 1968 they asked UNESCO to carry out a survey. An Anglo-French diving team discovered an extraordinary assemblage of statues, hieroglyphs and columns, and their report of 1975 concluded that the site at the foot of the Qait-Bey fort housed a priceless collection of treasures.

Egypt was facing financial difficulties, however, and excavation of the site would require massive funds which it was not in a position to release. Moreover, the city was undergoing rapid expansion and the most pressing need was to save those sites threatened by urbanisation. Protected by the sea, remains that had been submerged for thousands of years could clearly wait a little longer.

Fishing for clues

Alexandria's eastern harbour was the site of one of the largest Mediterranean sea ports of the ancient world, the Portus Magnus, which was finally destroyed by natural causes. The current harbour is a magnificent roadstead protected by two huge modern breakwaters, and is used by fishermen and yachtsmen. The project proposed by the IEASM consisted primarily in establishing the general topography of the submerged area. In 1990, a proposal was made to the Egyptian authorities in the following terms: "All the work accomplished by archaeologists endeavouring to establish a map of the bay, however brilliant, rests entirely on suppositions. Thanks to the technical resources now available to us we are able to assemble concrete information regarding the positioning of the monuments and substructures of the ancient harbour, and thereby establish a reliable map. These resources are unique. Only later, once we have drawn up the map, will we be in a position to undertake excavations and uncover traces of the life of the Ptolemies."

The Minister for Culture, Farouk Hosni, was in favour of the plan and the Director of Museums and Archaeological Sites of Alexandria expressed her undivided support for it. Since the harbour was situated in a military zone, we would be the only people working there.

One of Cleopatra's Needles at the time of its removal to New York, in 1879. The building immediately behind is still standing, enabling us to establish the original location of the obelisk.

Alexandria's eastern harbour as it is today. Faced with the smooth curve of the bay, who could guess the contours of the earlier coastline submerged beneath these waters?

View of the Portus Magnus. The survey area (covering the entire harbour) measures 4km² and represents the largest site of marine excavations to date.

Methodology

Armed with all the experience we had gained from previous excavations, we were nevertheless conscious of the enormity of the task that lay ahead. We proposed to tackle the site using the following procedures:

- an exhaustive geophysical survey over the entire area using non-invasive measures and production of maps on the basis of the information obtained, including

    magnetic readings,
    maps plotting the notable points detected by side scan sonar,
    bathymetric maps,
    geological maps indicating the different sedimentary strata and the scars caused by natural disasters;

- a campaign of geological core-drilling in order to produce geological maps by determining the nature of the geological strata;

- visual surveys of zones where notable anomalies were indicated by the use of different electronic instruments, including magnetometers, a side scan sonar, depth sounders and a sub-bottom profiler;

- production of maps of visible artefacts through differential correction (see p. 27) or acoustic positioning combined with the geophysical and geological survey maps;

- archaeological excavations aimed at identifying structures at notable points determined by analysis of the various maps and located by visual surveys;

- production of maps of recovered remains combined with the survey maps;

- following discussion with the scientific committee, complementary archaeological excavations at sites deemed to be priority sites.

This method of working may seem laborious, but we could not have proceeded any differently to achieve our objective – to arrive at a real topographical map of Alexandria's submerged areas.

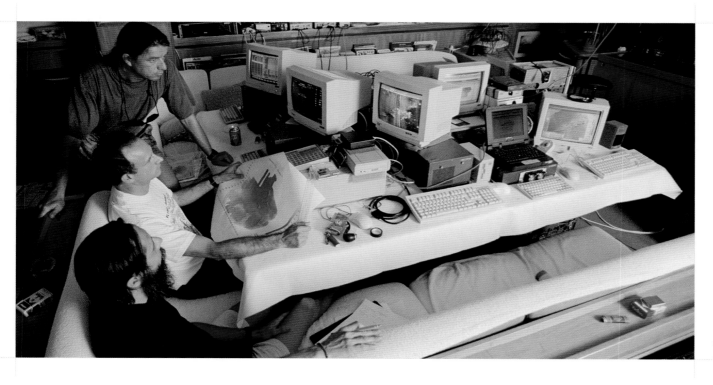

On board the search catamaran. Data collected on the sea-bed are processed by powerful computers.

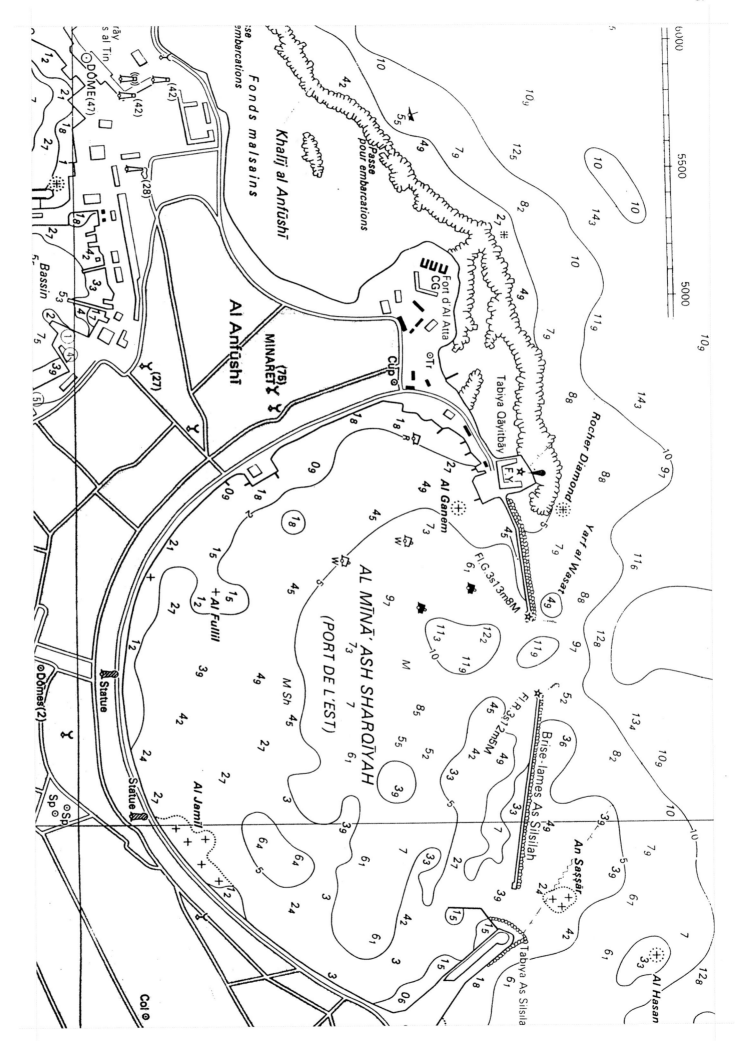

Current map of Alexandria's eastern harbour.

Underwater archaeological surveying and magnetometry

Gérard Schnepp,
engineer

The search for ancient wrecks and remains of classical antiquity is always preceded by lengthy archive studies which aim to determine the probable location and thus the best site for exploration.

The size of the search area finally selected depends on the historical context of the site and the interpretation of the data gleaned from the extensive archive investigations. It may be limited to a few square kilometres or extend over a vast area of ocean.

This area is then the object of a geophysical survey. The survey is conducted using different sensors to measure the physical characteristics of the site. The purpose of this is to reveal anomalies which may correspond to archaeological remains.

A boat, usually a catamaran, equipped with measuring instruments and computer systems for obtaining and processing information, systematically scours the entire search area along parallel lines (known as profiles) spaced 30–80m apart depending on the average depth of the site and the nature of the remains to be discovered. The catamaran is positioned in real time by a system of differential correction using satellites (DGPS).

Diagram showing detection systems.

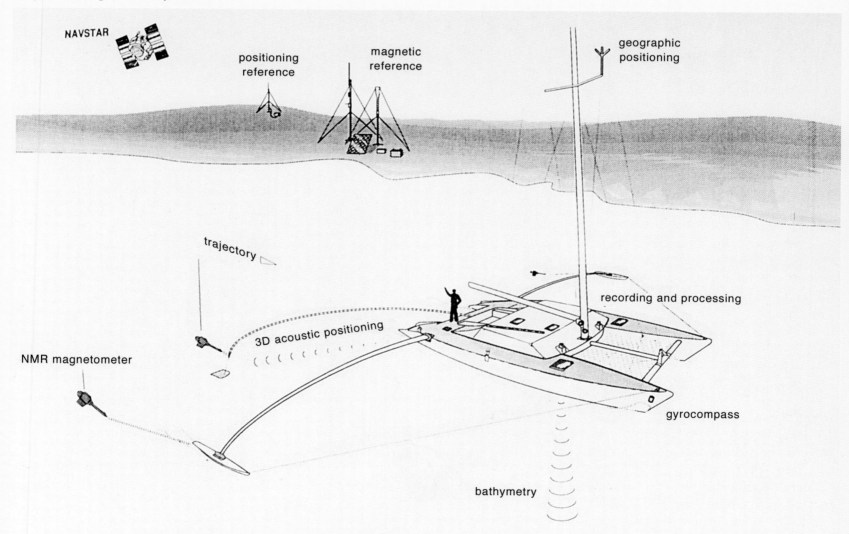

IGMMAR : Marine Magnetometry System for Geophysical Investigation

Nuclear magnetic resonance magnetometers (NMRs) and a side scan sonar, operated by means of electrical winches, are towed by the boat on the surface in shallow areas or submerged by hydrodynamic depressors in deeper water. A system of acoustic positioning continuously transmits the relative position of the sensors. The catamaran is also equipped with high-resolution echo sounders.

All the recorded parameters are subjected to an initial analysis in real time during the course of the survey. Daily processing of the data leads to the generation of bathymetric maps (showing a relief of the ocean bed) and magnetometric maps (showing magnetic fields) of the area under survey, completed by a sonar image of the sea-bed (using acoustic photography).

Analysis of these documents enables the exact position of the selected targets to be determined.

When an anomaly has been measured, experienced divers or remotely operated vehicles (ROVs) make an initial inspection in order to identify its origin. Even in clear water the remains of a wreck are rarely visible. The process of uncovering detected material, which is often buried or covered with thick deposits, generally requires soundings to be taken.

Survey vessel

A catamaran is often preferred to a mono-hull on account of its greater width and stability. Where necessary, it also permits the exploration of shallow areas due to its shallow draught. It is built of composite materials and its weak intrinsic magnetism does not interfere with magnetometric measurements, making it the ideal support boat for this kind of surveying.

Anomalies

The techniques of geophysical analysis consist of revealing the discontinuities of the parameters measured, such as the ambient magnetic field and the acoustic response of various terrains. These discontinuities or contrasts are called 'anomalies'.

In archaeological terms the range of interesting anomalies is very limited. The sensors also pick up numerous naturally occurring geological features which show up as anomalies. The discovery of remains depends on correctly differentiating between these two kinds of anomalies.

The success of this is dictated by the sensitivity of the sensors and their configuration, the processing of the data and the correlative analysis of the measurements taken by the various instruments.

NMR magnetometers

NMR magnetometers are the principal sensors in our surveying system. These high-resolution sensors were developed by the CEA (the French atomic energy commission). Based on the double magnetic resonance of protons and electrons (the Abragam-Overhauser effect), these NMR magnetometers measure the absolute value of the earth's magnetic field more than 1,000 times a second with a precision of a $50,000^{th}$ of its value.

Theory

The probe is a field/frequency transducer based on the principle of nuclear magnetic resonance amplified by dynamic electronic polarisation. The hydrogen atoms of standard solvents have a magnetic moment proportional to their spin. In the earth's magnetic field, they precess around this field at a frequency proportional to its modulus (called the Larmor frequency, from 1kHz to 3kHz within the earth's magnetic field).

The resonant electromagnetic excitation creates by spin phase coherence a macroscopic magnetic component precessing at the Larmor frequency. This component induces a voltage in the detection coil. The frequency measured gives the value of the magnetic field.

The nuclear magnetism thus created is not directly detectable in the measurement of the earth's magnetic field. The dynamic electronic polarisation amplifies the nuclear signal by a factor of 1,000. The nuclear spins are coupled to the free electron spins of a radical in solution. There are two possible frequencies of excitation of the electronic resonance: one generates a positive polarisation, the other a negative polarisation. The frequencies depend on the solvent used.

The judicious choice of a pair of solvents containing the same radical will give, at the same frequency, a positive polarisation factor in one of the solvents and a negative polarisation factor in the other. This is known as the double Abragam-Overhauser effect.

The probe is composed of two hydrogenated solvents in separate bottles containing a free radical in solution: a high-frequency dynamic polarisation excitation circuit and a low-frequency circuit which, respectively and simultaneously, excite the nuclear resonance and measure the signal. The probe, therefore, also comprises two symmetrical coils mounted in opposition to one another.

Geomagnetism

The earth's magnetic field superimposes highly complex temporal and spatial phenomena – geology of the earth's crust, dynamo effect, sun–earth interaction, circulation of ionospheric and telluric currents, etc. – involving magnetic and electrical properties.

The earth's magnetic field can be schematically considered as bipolar and of a value lying between 20,000 nanotesla (nT) at the equator and 60,000nT at the poles, in addition to which there exists a field of global anomalies (of the order of 10,000nT), a field of local anomalies of geological origins and temporary phenomena of some tens of nT every 24 hours.

Application to archaeology

The magnetic anomalies created by archaeological remains are superimposed on these anomalies of natural origin. The ability to differentiate between all these anomalies is based on the extreme sensitivity of our magnetometers and, where necessary, on the measurement of the local magnetic gradient between two sensors towed simultaneously. This gradient meter reduces in real time the temporal variations of the earth's magnetic field and enables us to dismiss a great many of the geological anomalies. This method, implemented using NMR magnetometers, permits the detection of objects with very weak magnetism, even when they are buried deep under layers of sediment.

Side scan sonar

This sensor delivers an acoustic image of the sea-bed in a band of 50–150m either side of the research ship. It reveals rocks and other prominent objects lying on the sea-bed and can give an indication of their size by measuring the shadow which they project. Magnetometers can simultaneously determine whether these targets are magnetic or not. By juxtaposing geographically positioned bands, the sonar information can be used to create a mosaic of the surveyed area.

Echo sounders

A precise relief map of the sea-bed is obtained using echo sounders. These acoustic sensors deliver continuous accurate depth measurements along the surveying profiles.

Differential positioning using satellites

GPS (Global Positioning System) is a method of absolute geographic positioning, providing across the whole of the earth's surface the position in latitude, longitude and altitude of a mobile receiver using information emitted by a constellation of satellites.

However, GPS can sometimes be inaccurate, with a margin of error of up to 100m. In order to achieve the submetric precision required by archaeological surveying, a method known as DGPS (Differential Global Positioning System) is implemented, whereby a reference station is set up on the ground which sends corrections in real time by radio to the mobile receiver.

System of acoustic positioning

Described as short base, this system relies on the regular emission of an acoustic signal by a transmitter (which is mounted on the mobile unit to be positioned) to a submerged receiver attached to the vessel. Several transmitters can be used simultaneously.

The position of each mobile unit is thus calculated in terms of range and bearing in relation to the receiver. Since the DGPS position of the vessel is already known, the precise geographical location of each sensor equipped with an acoustic transmitter can therefore be determined in real time.

Data acquisition and processing

The survey catamaran is equipped with computer systems for data acquisition and navigation, which record the information from the geophysical sensors (magnetometers, echo sounders and side scan sonar, etc.) and the sensors recording positioning and altitude (GPS, acoustic positioning systems, submerged magnetometers, magnetic course).

This vessel-based system of processing enables us to create maps from the survey results and analyse all the various elements of the geophysical investigations.

Left: Magnetic reference and GPS receiver, Qait-Bey fort.

Below: Magnetic detectors seen from the survey vessel during the 1997 survey.

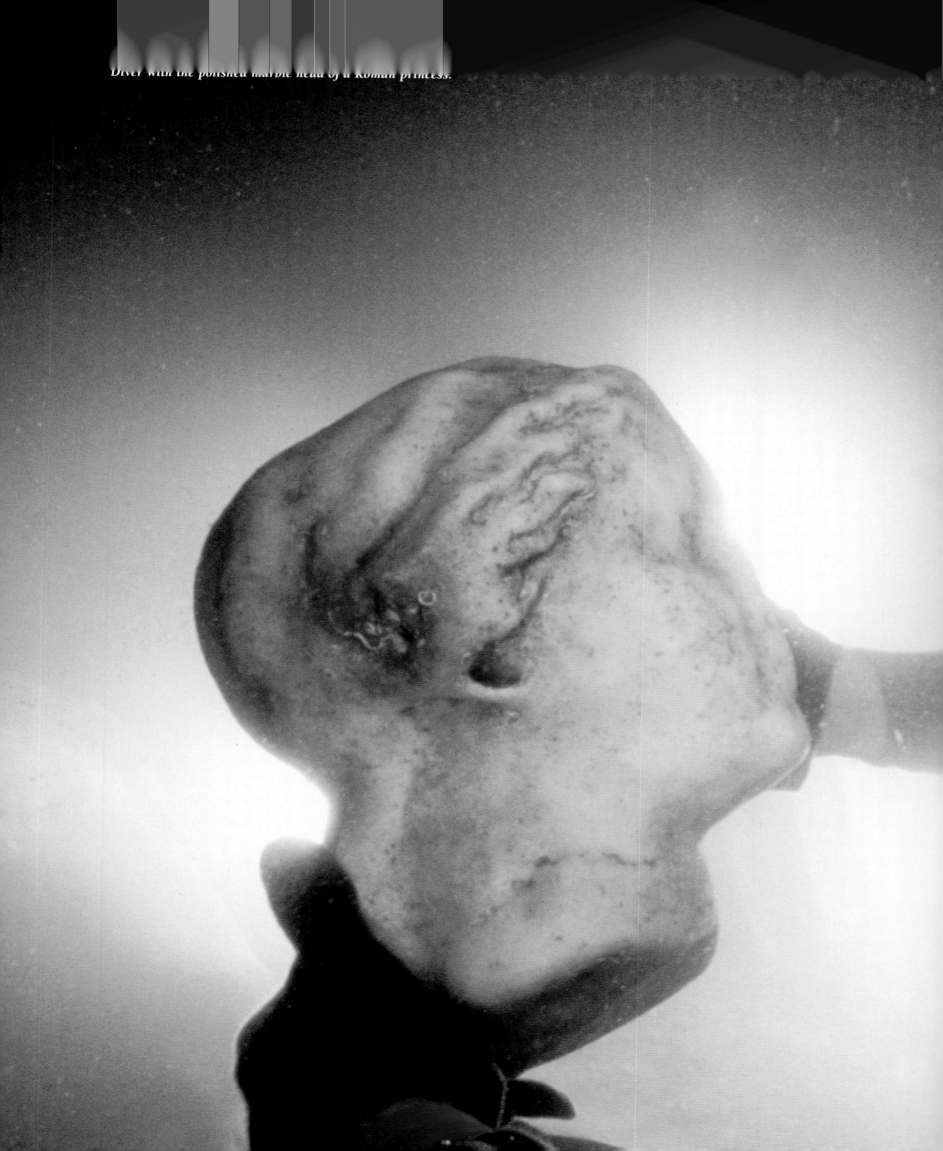

Diver with the polished marble head of a Roman princess.

Members of the team conferring on board the support boat, the Princess Duda. The divers are due to survey a new site of potential interest indicated by the electronic maps.

Team and logistics

Underwater archaeology demands an historical approach, knowledge of the sea and mastery of excavation techniques specific to the marine environment, as well as technical expertise and even manual skills. It can only be carried out by a team of experts working in collaboration with one another.

Such a multi-disciplinary team will include archaeologists, ceramics experts, numismatists, palaeoanthropologists, epigraphers with specialist knowledge of a number of ancient languages, historians, electronics engineers, geophysicists, specialists in restoration and conservation, divers specialising in archaeological work, photographers, film-makers and sailors. Since underwater communications are fraught with difficulties, the experience of the excavators and their ability to work together are determining factors in the success of such investigations. The members of the European Institute of Marine Archaeology (IEASM) team have been working together for many years, engaged in operations of several months' duration. Hence their intimate understanding of underwater sites and their ability to coordinate their working methods in a way that has proved invaluable.

The presence of support boats, surveying instruments and, in the case of deep-water excavations, submarines or remotely operated vehicles (ROVs), can convert a marine excavation into a major work site.

Excavations of Alexandria's eastern harbour involved a team of 35 people, supported by 28 crew members, working on site.

Carrying out the underwater investigations, and supporting this on-board community for a period of several months, was inevitably a complex and costly operation, but the success of the excavations largely depended on it.

The vessels used included a 45m-long support boat – enabling the team to live above the site, so minimising transport and intervention time – together with an electronically equipped survey boat, three small runabouts and a communications tender.

There was also an office on the mainland.

A converted fishing boat used for soundings and pinpoint excavations.

The Princess Duda is not just a boat, more of a floating community, housing a team of some 30 individuals for the duration of the mission.

A block of pink granite inscribed with hieroglyphs, seen shortly after it had been cleaned of its deposits. A silicone membrane will be used to produce an impression of the hieroglyphs, which can then be deciphered.

Material and equipment

An isothermal suit protects the diver against the cold and minor injuries such as cuts or scrapes. The suit, which is made to measure in a heavy-duty red neoprene, is equipped with a hood and an inner lining made of titanium, which is 40% more effective in reducing heat loss than a conventional suit. The suit may be 'wet' (in which case a thin stream of water circulates between the material and the wearer's body, heating up in contact with the skin) or completely waterproof, but in either case its buoyancy is counteracted by a weighted belt (between 6 and 10kg) which enables the wearer to move about on the sea-bed with relative ease. A pair of

**Bernard Camier,
head of logistics**

gloves covered in kevlar and a pair of neoprene ankle boots are other indispensable items.

Two connected heavy steel cylinders of compressed air, 12 litres apiece, filled at a pressure of 200 bars, provide 4.8m³ total

volume of air, which is designed to last for three to four hours depending on the diver's activity. These cylinders are attached to a heavily inflatable vest which is supplied with air from the cylinders. This vest guarantees the diver's safety at all levels of his dive and also helps him to maintain his balance underwater and to shift heavy loads. Each diver breathes into a so-called two-stage regulator, which delivers air on demand. By glancing at his manometer (pressure gauge), he can continuously regulate his consumption of air and so exercise greater control over his dive.

Movement through the water is facilitated by the use of high-performance flippers. A mask is also worn and is specially designed to fit the wearer's face so that the water does not come into contact with his skin – an important consideration in areas of heavy pollution. The mask also enables the diver to communicate with his colleagues on the surface and so report directly on any discoveries he might make.

Other indispensable accessories include a knife to cut himself free if he becomes entangled in a fishing net; an underwater compass to guide him and locate the alignments of buried structures; an electronic depth gauge in order to ascertain the precise depth of any finds; and finally a lamp to illuminate the outlines of such objects and to help him decipher potential inscriptions.

Diver, kitted out and ready for action, in Alexandria's eastern harbour.

The sounding and excavation material

Whenever a diver makes an inspection he uses a pick and a scraper, both made of stainless steel, to examine deposits and scrape free any archaeological finds. He takes measurements using a decametre and records his findings on a plastic slate, then marks the position of the archaeological material with a numbered red buoy. The geographical coordinates (latitude and longitude) of the buoy are recorded using DGPS and entered on a general site map. Divers then install on the seabed a two-dimensional grid reference system (using x and y coordinates), which covers the area selected for excavation. This consists of two

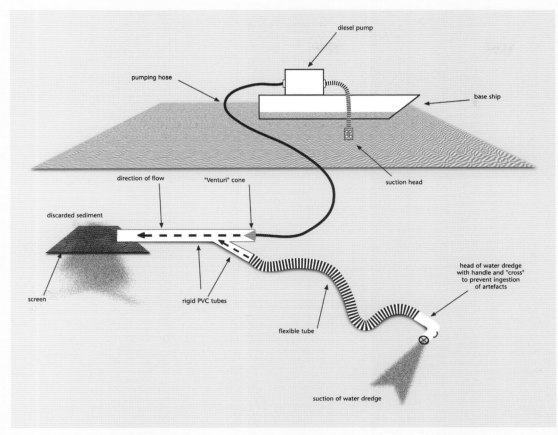

Diagram showing how a water dredge works.

These boats usually have two dredges and a pump on board.

Logistics

"The success of our missions depends on the organisation and effective use of the material," says Bernard Camier. "First of all, the equipment is chosen to suit the excavation objectives and the budget. We have to find a good supplier, adapt the material to our working conditions and transport it to Alexandria, by plane or boat, before the start of the mission. By pooling the experience and ideas of each member of the team, we are constantly modifying the apparatus so as to improve its performance and make it easier and safer to use. This goes for the dredges and diving suits, and for everything else for that matter, pumps, diving accessories, etc. I am also responsible for hiring some of the equipment (the crane and the boats, for example) on site and recruiting the personnel along with it.

"The *Princess Duda* is like a small floating town. Supplies have to be organised on a daily basis and the equipment needs to be maintained, and inventoried and stored between missions.

"And I am responsible for getting the entire team to the excavation site – plane tickets, insurance, made-to-measure suits – not to mention dealing with the Egyptian authorities over excavation permits."

perpendicular nylon baselines held in place at either end by stainless steel pegs and with the metres marked off using numbers or letters.

The third dimension is supplied by a small gantry which can be moved horizontally on rails at a fixed reference height as the excavation proceeds. The sediment is then removed using a water dredge, which works by the Venturi effect (see diagram). This light plastic dredge is swiftly assembled in situ and supplied with water under pressure (2–3 bars) by a diesel-run motor pump situated at the surface. A fine mesh screen is placed at the mouth of the dredge in order to collect any small artefacts which the diver may have missed.

The boats

The *Princess Duda*, a former coasting vessel, serves as a base for personnel and equipment. The boat is securely anchored on six concrete moorings, just above the main excavation site, and remains in position whatever the weather conditions. On board there is a compressor for filling the diving tanks, a crane and a spacious deck where the archaeological material can be housed

and initial conservation measures taken. During operations, around 30 people sleep, eat and work on the boat. For pinpoint excavations or soundings, the team use several sturdy motorised fishing boats, hired along with their crew in the port of Alexandria.

Final adjustments before rejoining the world of silence.

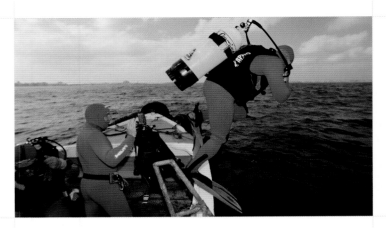

The start of a two-hour dive, repeated twice daily, morning and afternoon.

This underwater DGPS, used for the first time in archaeology, enables divers to trace the contour of submerged coastlines.

Methodology of underwater excavations

Although it shares the same objectives as terrestrial archaeology, underwater archaeology uses different techniques and materials specific to underwater conditions.

The water dredge

This instrument is indispensable to underwater excavations. It relies on the Venturi effect, obtained by injecting pressurised water into a tube, the size of which, together with the pressure used, can be adapted to suit different tasks. (A variant technique utilises the expansion of air injected under pressure, but this can often be harder to control.) The excavator holds the instrument about 20cm above the sediment, while gently fanning the latter with his free hand: the sediment is sucked into the tube and discarded at a distance via waste pipes. A screen, positioned over the outlet, is designed to collect any objects that may have been sucked in by accident – something that rarely occurs if the excavator is experienced.

The diameter of the tube is not particularly important in controlling the process; the relevant factors are the flow and the pressure of the jet of water responsible for the Venturi effect. Some excavators prefer small diameters, whilst others feel more comfortable working with larger diameters coupled with a weak jet.

The advantage of this method lies in the fact that the material under excavation does not come into contact with the instrument. An experienced excavator is able to exercise precise control over the vacuumed material, separating the most minute and fragile objects from the sediment without causing them any damage. Over the years, the IEASM team has perfected a number of variants operated by submerged electric pumps whose use has now been adopted by a great many underwater archaeologists.

Labelling

Divers are supplied with nylon nets or plastic pockets of varying sizes, each bearing a polyester label attached to a loop with a plastic tie. These labels have the identification code of the excavation printed on them in indelible ink. Each item recovered is placed in its own individual nylon net, and the diver records the following information in pencil on the label:

- the position of the object in terms of latitude, longitude and altitude, to be converted into coordinates (x, y, z);
- the identifying mark of the person responsible for finding the object;
- the azimuth of the object (that is, its compass orientation, measured in degrees);
- the angle of the object from the vertical, from 0 to 90°.

The nets are collected and placed in plastic boxes weighted with lead, which are then raised to the surface.

The water dredge is designed to remove sediment from an excavation site by working in one small area at a time. It is being used here around a cannon discovered on one of Napoleon's ships, part of the fleet that sank at Aboukir in 1798.

The position of each archaeological find is systematically recorded, as here, in terms of latitude and longitude, followed by its orientation and angle: valuable information which serves as a basis for a general plan of the archaeological site and its subsequent interpretation.

A new life in the fresh air

Once it reaches the surface, an object is taken in hand by specialists in conservation and restoration. After being gently cleaned in sea water, it is returned to its net, and the date of its discovery is entered on the label. It is then transferred to a desalination tank.

This tank is filled with a mixture of 50% sea water and 50% fresh water in order to avoid any deterioration due to violent osmosis. After several days in this bath, the object, still in its net, is submerged in a second bath of fresh water which is continuously renewed and the salinity of the bath is measured to determine when the object can be retrieved and dried without damage. Later, on land, it will be exposed to a more complete desalination process using distilled water. Organic materials are also treated later, and while on board are simply kept in a damp environment.

The object is then described, measured and inventoried, and a second label bearing the inventory number is attached to the net. This label is also pre-printed by computer on polyester paper using indelible ink, in order to avoid the risk of skipping numbers or misreading information. The details are then entered on to a database with the corresponding photos.

The strict application of this procedure is essential. Otherwise information could easily be lost, given the number of stages between the discovery of an artefact and its final restoration, when it can be labelled in Indian ink on a thin layer of white varnish.

Column capital being carefully measured after the removal of ancient deposits. A more rigorous examination will follow once it has been raised to the surface.

Artefacts recovered in the course of excavations – here the neck of an amphora – are put in nets each bearing a number, and these are stowed in plastic boxes ready to be lifted up to the surface.

Initial conservation measures: desalination. As soon as it reaches the surface, the archaeological material is immersed in basins containing a mixture of fresh and salt water to gradually remove salts by a process of osmosis.

*Desalination is carried out in tanks like these, on the upper deck of the support vessel, the **Princess Duda**. The process of desalination is followed by painstaking restoration work in the laboratory.*

A portable 50cm² grid is laid within the overall 1m² site grid, allowing for more accurate plotting of areas of particular significance.

Grid reference system

How do you reproduce precisely on a plan the position of objects discovered during an excavation? Traditionally by dividing the excavation site into squares with the aid of ropes or cables which serve as reference points. This system, known as a grid reference, enables us to provide each object with a set of coordinates determining its position. Another method uses the underwater GPS system developed by the IEASM or acoustic underwater positioning systems.

Underwater or on land, the principles of a grid are the same: in either instance a series of chains, ropes or cables are extended to form a grid and firmly anchored in the ground. The difference is that under water the grid can pose a hazard. The diver is unable to control his own movements, at the mercy of the waves, the swell and the currents. His greatest fear is that he may become accidentally entangled with an obstacle and not be able to free himself in time should his oxygen start to run out or some other emergency occur – all it takes is for a clasp to overshoot its mark and become enmeshed in the spider's web of cables. It is worth remembering that visibility beneath the surface is sometimes so poor that the diver can hardly see further than his own nose. There are obvious advantages, therefore, in using a mobile grid system, which slides over the reference lines. Such a system requires an absolute minimum of fixed lines firmly anchored in the ocean bed and therefore presents fewer risks for the diver.

A preferred option is the electronic method. Over a limited area, modern methods of acoustic positioning (underwater DGPS) achieve a degree of precision that can be measured in centimetres, and these methods have all but superseded the fixed grid system. The installation of a grid using physical reference points will be limited in future to helping the diver determine his own position, particularly in conditions of poor visibility, rather than determining the precise location of artefacts.

Finally, some coordinates, as for example in surveys of naval architecture, are easier to map using the method of triangulation, starting from fixed reference points in space and relying on the use of a measuring tape or decametre (instruments familiar to both underwater and terrestrial archaeologists).

An underwater excavation site needs a minimum of fixed reference lines spaced at intervals which will be determined by its size and depth, the currents and the ambient visibility. In Alexandria's eastern harbour, local references were positioned wherever excavations were carried out, and an orthogonal grid was installed on the excavation site. Because the point of origin and the direction of each baseline is precisely located within the geographical system, it becomes possible (using a series of mathematical calculations) to automatically convert all the data collected at each specific reference point of the excavation. The data can therefore be interpreted either in geographical terms or in relation to the reference point.

A diver records the position of excavated material in relation to the grid.

Back at the surface, each object is marked on the excavation plan (shown here), and as excavations proceed a general overview of the archaeological site emerges, providing a basis for expert interpretation.

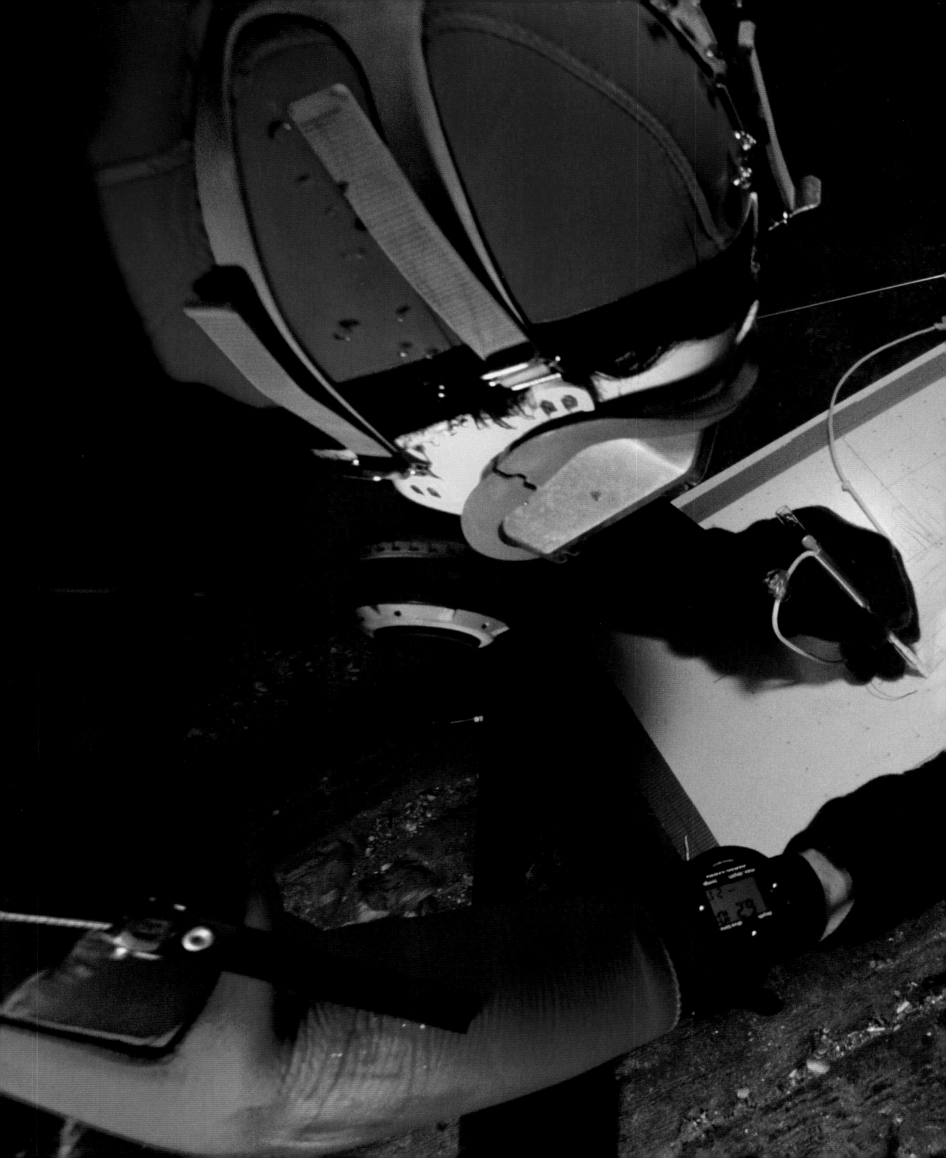

The efforts of divers like this one – spending hour after hour, day after day, measuring, describing and drawing – are rewarded as Alexandria's ancient contours gradually emerge.

The excavation plan

**Patrice Sandrin,
draughtsman**

Given the objective of our mission – to produce a topographical survey – Patrice Sandrin, as the team's draughtsman, occupied a key position. Sandrin is passionate about archaeology and whenever the team re-groups he leaves his bookshop in the Doubs and joins forces with us. Thanks to his gift for draughtsmanship, he is able to represent the underwater terrain in precise terms prior to any attempt at interpretation.

The archaeological site is divided into 1m-sized squares which make up what we call the grid. My work consists of reproducing this grid on a piece of paper and drawing the objects in exactly the same positions. As the excavation proceeds, I mark on a plan the archaeological material uncovered by the excavators, who have already given each object a label indicating its position, its orientation and its elevation at a previously defined reference point. For extensive sites or surveys of naval architecture, I often practise the method of triangulation, using three double decametres extended from fixed points. Three posts accessible from every point of the site are precisely positioned using GPS. I then extend a decametre from each post towards the point to be mapped and note the distances on my slate.

Back on board, I transfer these three measurements on to my plan to the required scale using a pair of compasses. If I have measured accurately, the three arcs should intersect at the same point, marking the position of the object. If the arcs do not quite intersect, there is no alternative but to repeat the measurements at the next dive. I also note the length, width and height (or diameter) of every construction block and column reclaimed by the excavators. A protractor also calculates its angle, and an underwater compass its orientation. Any unusually shaped material (statues, column capitals, etc.) is systematically brought up to the surface and carefully drawn.

Down on the bottom I write all the measurements I have collected with a pencil on a large plastic slate covered with a sheet of transparent polyester. The written sheets are called 'excavation minutes'. The poor visibility in the harbour at Alexandria complicates matters. At each triangulation I am obliged to keep returning to the three points of origin to check that my measuring tapes were positioned correctly, since if the tapes become twisted or tangled this will completely distort the measurements. In these conditions, when the weather is calm, I can plot the position of some 25 artefacts during a two-hour dive. But the work becomes impossible when visibility drops below 50cm or when there is a strong current or swell.

Back on the boat, I lay out a large-format polyester sheet on my drawing board. This is the excavation plan. First, I put in the baselines, before drawing the archaeological material with the help of those precious excavation minutes (which are then filed). I use three pairs of compasses, a ruler, a protractor and a pencil. The excavation plan is built up in this way, day by day, until a complete picture of the archaeological site emerges, enabling us to understand and interpret it better. On the Poseidium peninsula, for example, we had begun to locate a number of construction blocks, but very bad visibility made it impossible

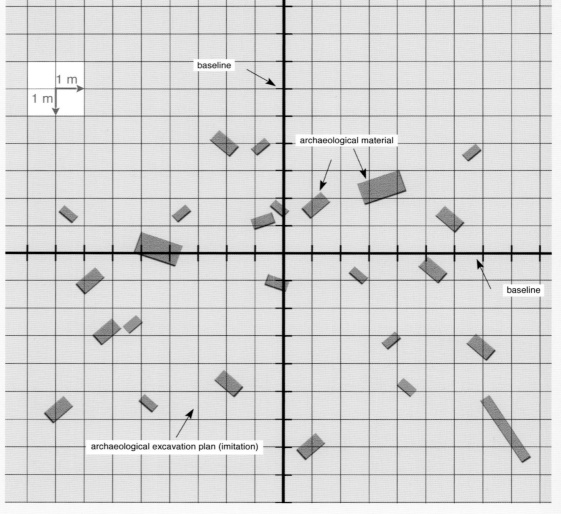

baseline

archaeological material

1 m

1 m

baseline

archaeological excavation plan (imitation)

Sketch plan of a grid frame.

to gain any kind of overall view. Then, on the plan, little by little, we saw the outlines of an enormous building (whose precise dimensions we can calculate today) appearing before our eyes. What a surprise that was, and what a reward for all those long diving hours!

Once the mission is complete, I make a fair copy of the excavation plan in ink, including the necessary references, and this document provides a basic source of information for the experts whose job it will be to interpret the discoveries.

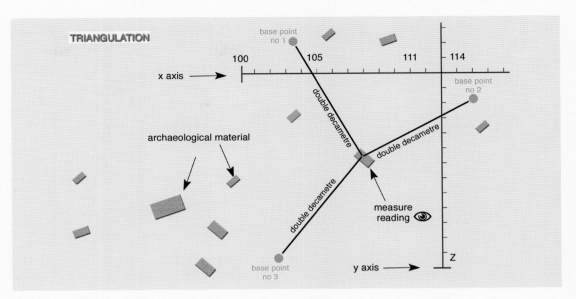

Diagram showing the positioning of archaeological material using the method known as triangulation.

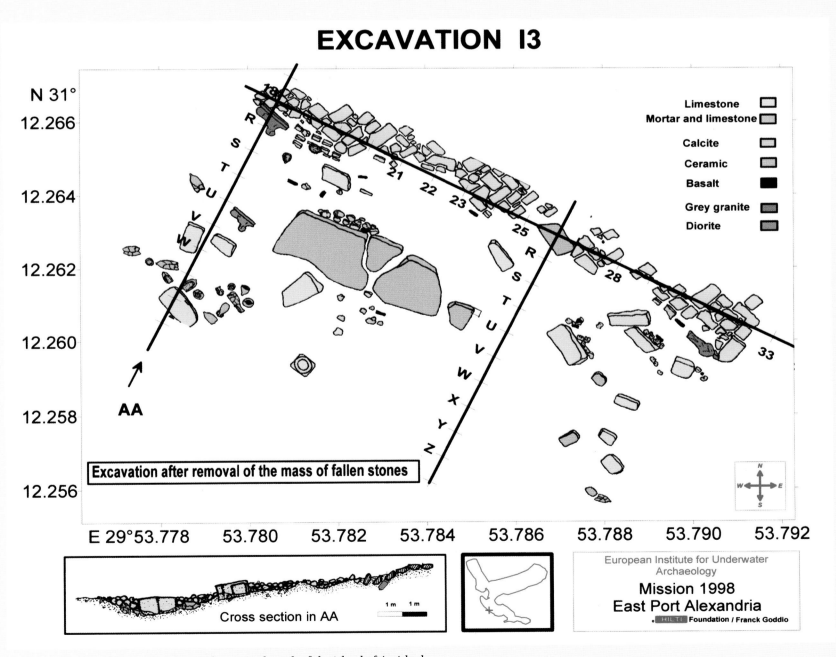

EXCAVATION I3

Excavation after removal of the mass of fallen stones

Cross section in AA

European Institute for Underwater Archaeology
**Mission 1998
East Port Alexandria**
HILTI Foundation / Franck Goddio

Legend:
- Limestone
- Mortar and limestone
- Calcite
- Ceramic
- Basalt
- Grey granite
- Diorite

Finalised plan of excavations on the south-western branch of the island of Antirhodos.

Divers recording the position of individual objects.

Heavy objects are lifted using special balloons and systematically turned so that they can be examined from every angle. This can sometimes reveal ancient inscriptions that were previously invisible.

All in a day's work

The secret of a well run excavation site resides with the team itself: its professionalism and enthusiasm, and the solidarity of its members. From year to year this team of people will intermittently re-group and then disband once a mission has been completed. The ability to communicate is paramount, and under water this depends entirely on gestures rather than words. All the necessary procedures have to be in place and everything is carefully planned – everything, that is, except the discoveries themselves.

Weather conditions at sea can change very suddenly and sometimes impose strict constraints on the work of the team. This is why excavations are always carried out at a time of year when the climate is most favourable and why they rarely continue for longer than two months at a stretch. The entire team of 20 or 30 (depending on the mission) live on the boat during that time.

First stage: locating the position of the buoys

Every minute is precious at sea and we are up every day at 6am, working by 7am. The two engineers responsible for locating the position of the buoys using GPS are the first over the rails. They board a rubber dinghy equipped with a high-performance differential correction system or DGPS (see p. 27) and site the GPS antenna just above the buoys (positioned by the divers the previous day). Each of these buoys has a number and acts as a marker for a submerged structure or a set of artefacts. The precise position of each buoy is calculated while the mooring line is held steady so that it rises vertically from the point to be located. Since the numbers of the buoys have already been recorded, together with the material which they are marking, all that remains is to correlate the positions of the buoys with the identified objects in order to complete the plan.

Diving – for better or for worse

Teams of divers systematically explore predefined search areas and if they detect any artefacts they mark their positions with buoys before extricating the buried material from its layers of deposits. This is the main focus of their work, and also the most interesting part – guessing what may lie concealed behind formless blocks of stone, constantly on the look-out for traces of the past. Dressed in red diving suits, they go down in pairs, wearing heavy cylinders of compressed air on their backs. They breathe through face masks which protect their faces from pollution: the depth of the site rarely exceeds 6m, but the harbour waters in Alexandria are very dirty, since the sewers drain directly into them. Dirty water is, as it happens, the major concern of this particular site since it is often no longer possible even to see one's own hands under water here. The divers carry out two dives a day, each of approximately two hours' duration, often groping their way around with their nose pressed to the compass. In such conditions it is difficult not to get lost.

In order to complete the mapping process begun by the engineers, two diver-draughtsmen take measurements of each find, which are transferred the same day on to a scale plan of the survey. On the basis of this information another set of divers install a grid frame on a site which the archaeologists have assessed as potentially interesting to excavate, before beginning the laborious task of removing sediment using water dredges. Heavier objects are sometimes lifted by means of a balloon or crane, and where inscriptions are present silicone moulds are made *in situ*. Each find is photographed by a specialist photographer, who is also responsible for taking the photographs destined to appear in scientific journals – the final chapter of an excavation. The divers are also sometimes accompanied by film crews making documentaries.

Work on board

After two hours of working on the seabed the divers are relieved by a new team. Back at the surface they make a detailed report of the work they have carried out. The information is written up in an excavation notebook and the position of artefacts is entered on the excavation plan. As the drawing becomes more and more detailed a general view of the site gradually emerges, as if the sediment were disappearing by magic, and the process of interpretation can begin.

Meanwhile, on deck, a small group of people are busy cleaning and rinsing the archaeological objects that have been retrieved, before submerging them in a series of freshwater baths to remove the salt. Each object is then measured, described, numbered, drawn, photographed and indexed before being handed over to the inspectors of the Egyptian Supreme Council for Antiquities who monitor our missions. A restorer carries out initial conservation work, a moulding specialist takes impressions of objects carrying inscriptions (making it a great deal easier to read and understand them) and a ceramics expert examines the pottery. This is the moment when the first hypotheses are put forward, and from now on each day provides a new piece to the jigsaw puzzle.

The archaeological material is labelled and photographed in situ. A levelling rod (in this case, a chequered ruler) gives an idea of its dimensions. All measurements, positions and photographs are entered into a database.

... and living en famille

Mealtimes are welcome get-togethers uniting the different members of the team: divers, researchers, engineers, but also the entire technical team in charge of the maintenance of the diving and excavation equipment. Despite the difficult working conditions, discussions are frequently animated and every new discovery is a source of great excitement. After dinner a brief meeting is held for the purpose of organising the following day's programme and communicating the results of analyses and the specialists' opinions regarding material so far recovered. Work continues late into the night for those whose job is to input the information on computer. This information is brought up to date twice a day and used to generate the various site maps, which are made available to the archaeologists the following morning.

Objects destined for further examination at the surface are stowed in plastic boxes.

The excavation notebook

This is a large black spiral-bound exercise book, in which every operation is written up and every day described in detail. In the middle of the cover is a sticking plaster with the drawing of a skull scrawled between exclamation marks – announcing to all and sundry that this is the "director's pencil!" Pencils easily go missing on board, and the director always likes to write with the same one!

By 7.30am the tasks have been allocated. Eric will be clearing sediment with the water dredge. The indefatigable Jean-Claude will be moving some giant blocks. He is not fazed by the prospect of spending eight hours in the water (double the usual daily diving time) and is sure to be the last one back. These men each have their speciality and all share an undying passion for underwater archaeology. It is this that gives them their staying power. Very often we find nothing. Fragments, perhaps, vague trails that lead nowhere, and sometimes nothing at all for weeks on end. Besides which there are days when diving is out of the question, when the swell becomes dangerous and visibility is down to a few centimetres. We generally stay on board then, fiddling with the maps and cleaning equipment contaminated by water pollution. Sometimes we dive anyway, blindly: we might as well have our eyes closed, and all that guides us is a kind of intuition located in our fingertips.

We need plenty of intuition. Despite all our sophisticated equipment, a moment comes when we have to make a decision: do we dive here, or there, or somewhere else? These excavations are like searching for a needle in a haystack. When we fix the perimeter of our search we may be missing – perhaps by centimetres – a fascinating object, buried in silt for thousands of years and destined to remain there for thousands more. There comes a time, nevertheless, when you have to trust your own instinct. This is where the director of excavations exercises his particular talents, guiding the efforts of the team. Why scrape this block of stone rather than that one? Well, perhaps because there is something about its shape, and in particular the sound it makes when struck: a peculiar resonance which suggests that a sculpture may well be hiding behind the coral. All the hours spent dredging sediment and scraping away several dozen centimetres of deposits with a trowel are sometimes fruitless – and sometimes amply rewarded.

The day of 7 October 1997 began like any other. The jobs were allocated to the various teams, who would come back for lunch before diving again, informing Franck of their discoveries … or their lack of discoveries. Since finding nothing, the director assures them, is finding that there is nothing; it is another way of completing the map, if only with blank spaces. Sometimes it is difficult to raise morale when the team is desperate to lay its hands on a piece of concrete evidence, a sign that the search is not a complete waste of time. The 7th, however, was a day when the Egyptian gods were generous with such signs.

Jean-Claude Roubaud, in charge of the divers and one of the team's greatest strengths.

7 October 1997 (extract)

Poor visibility. Sea pretty rough. Wind from the north-north-west.

Fernand and Bernard continuing excavations at the far end of the island. Alignment of wooden piles & large pink granite column buried in sand (6m long). Next to a wooden post, a small marble block with some Greek letters. Gregory joins them, measures the column and draws it.

Éric, Mohammed and Mostafa working on the secondary branch of the island. Morning: find chunks of basalt. Some appear to have been worked. Maybe fragments of a statue? The whole area is scattered with bits of paving which are beginning to cave in towards the south-west.

Daniel and Jean-Claude continuing excavations at the entrance to the secondary branch, determining the contours by positioning buoys. The point of the island is taking on a definite shape. The whole surface of this branch is covered with limestone slabs, some of them still in place (average dimensions: 25 x 80 x 50). Some in very good condition.

Gerard and Jean-Jacques are measuring GPS positions with the Zodiac: 32 points recorded. Carried over on to the plan.

2.30pm, the waves have come up. Very overcast weather.

Daniel joins Éric's team. They discover a grey granite sphinx near the RY5 point surrounded by paving, small blocks of grey granite and large blocks of limestone. Some of the blocks have slipped and smashed some amphorae: good opportunity for dating. This area of the island appears to have experienced subsidence. Large masses of ancient mortar 1m thick are broken on the flat part of the island. Some of them have slid down the slope with the material.

Éric discovers a new sphinx, very beautiful, in black diorite. Mostafa, 20m away, an extraordinary statue in grey granite. Figure carrying a Canopic vase with Osiris emerging from it. The faces are intact. The statue's head is shaved; its two fists are held together; tunic beautifully executed. The sphinx is lying on its right side. Its face seems to be intact. The extremity of its forepaws is broken. The statue of the priest is lying on its back; only its feet and the base are missing. Drawings. Co-ordinates noted. Photos.

It's 5pm. Slanting light. Everyone has a turn at diving so that they can see our new find. Emily Teeter stays on board. From the description, Emily is quite certain: it's a priest carrying a Canopic vase. Dive with the camera: it's dark and it's late. Bernand looks at the images: the statue is as beautiful as the one from Naples with the head missing.

We need to make a careful note of everything before we put it back. Bernard has done a good job clearing the surrounding area and doesn't think there was a pillar. The priest looks magical under the water.

High-tech underwater cartography
of the harbour at Alexandria

What did the ancient harbour of Alexandria look like? What were the broad outlines of its architecture before it was engulfed by the sea?

"To gain an idea of this we began by consulting all the available ancient texts, including those of the Greek geographer Strabo, written *circa* 27 BC, shortly after the death of Cleopatra," explains Gérard Schnepp. He and his colleague Jean-Jacques Groussard are the engineers on the Goddio team, both members of the CEA (the French atomic energy commission).

The two engineers and a team of technicians set out in a search catamaran, piloted by DGPS, and ploughed up and down the Bay of Alexandria, towing magnetometers, familiarly known as 'electronic fish'.

On board they operated a side scan sonar, a kind of submersible 'acoustic camera', which delivers exceptionally clear screen images of the sea-bed. Two NMR magnetometers (directly based on anti-submarine technology) were also used to show up the most minute anomaly, and an echo sounder (depth indicator) supplied bathymetric measurements of the site. The data were collected by powerful onboard computers and synthesised in the form of maps.

"Since we began our research in 1992, we have been drawing lines every 10m east to west and north to south over the entire surface area of the harbour, 4km^2 in total," confirm Gérard Schnepp and Jean-Jacques Groussard from behind their computer screens. "And we have seen the contours of the ancient landscape emerging, dramatic breakwaters and quays and a great many other remnants which could not have occurred completely naturally.

"These maps were later confirmed by lengthy diving searches in conditions of limited visibility. Equipped with underwater DGPS, divers were able to give us the real and definitive picture of the Portus Magnus as sailors in antiquity would have seen it.

"This high-tech underwater cartography of the harbour at Alexandria challenges the ideas of previous archaeologists, which

**Gérard Schnepp,
engineer**

were founded principally on the ancient texts."

The island of Antirhodos

The new underwater maps revealed a single island (1) situated in the south-east part of the harbour at an approximate depth of 6m. This island is 350m long by 70m wide and is made up of three branches. Some important finds were made, mainly on the island's principal branch (which is oriented south-west/north-east), including some impressive construction blocks, numerous alignments of columns and statue bases, regularly laid paving stones and wooden foundation posts, carbon dated to the 3rd century BC. It is quite possible to attribute these discoveries to the royal residence seen by Strabo shortly after the death of Cleopatra.

The small private harbour (2) also mentioned by the Greek geographer must have been located where the main branch and the southern branch form an angle on the lee side of the island (and where an ancient wreck has already been studied). The underwater map of the ancient harbour confirms the island's central position in the Portus Magnus, and its potentially key position in relation to the city.

Poseidium and Timonium

Immediately to the east of the island there is a large peninsula (3), approximately 350m long and 150m wide. Limestone blocks recently uncovered here belong to the foundations of a large building, possibly the Poseidium temple mentioned by

Strabo. The underwater maps also show that this large peninsula was extended by a series of breakwaters, one of which ends in a platform strewn with the remains of imposing structures (4). This must have been the Timonium, Mark Antony's private retreat (since there is no other site where it could reasonably have been located), and the date of remains found in the course of excavations confirms this hypothesis.

The harbour basins

Protected by a series of natural reefs (8) that are submerged today, the configuration of island and peninsula offered a perfect haven for navigators in antiquity. This harbour (5), the most important in the Portus Magnus, forms a parallelogram measuring approximately 500m by 320m, which amounts to a surface area of 16 hectares. Its principal entrance, situated between the eastern point of the island (1) and the Timonium platform (4), measured 80m in width. Protected from the open sea and orientated towards the prevailing winds, it provided easy access for sailing vessels.

A second, narrower channel (40m wide), situated between the southern point of the island (2) and the ancient coastline (6), offered an ideal exit for ships, and a perfect control point for the harbour authorities.

Immediately to the east of the Poseidium peninsula there is a second large port (7), 500m long by 500m wide (an area of 15 hectares), whose entrance, to the north-west, was protected from waves and swell by outlying reefs (8). These two harbours were clearly used for commercial purposes, a fact that is confirmed by the hundreds of amphorae in various styles that have been found buried in the silt.

The ancient texts also speak of a famous harbour *dug by human hands and closed off, for the private use of kings* (9), situated alongside Cape Lochias (0), where the Ptolemies had their palaces. It was here, in this harbour, that Julius Caesar set fire to his own fleet as a strategy for motivating his legions. This royal harbour, located on the extreme eastern side of the Portus

Magnus, alongside what is now a military zone, is due to be excavated in the near future.

Finally, other harbour basins (10 and 11) have also been located on the western side of the Portus Magnus, in an area where the ancient texts situate Alexandria's shipyards.

The ancient coastline

Happily for archaeologists, the submerged coastline (6) was not entirely built over during development in the 19th and 20th centuries. Underwater cartographic surveys show that the south-east coast of the Portus Magnus is still visible to divers. Its dramatic outline enables us to appreciate the shape of the different harbour basins and to gain an idea of their functions, while the numerous remains discovered in the course of pinpoint excavations confirm the importance of monuments erected along the length of this ancient coastline.

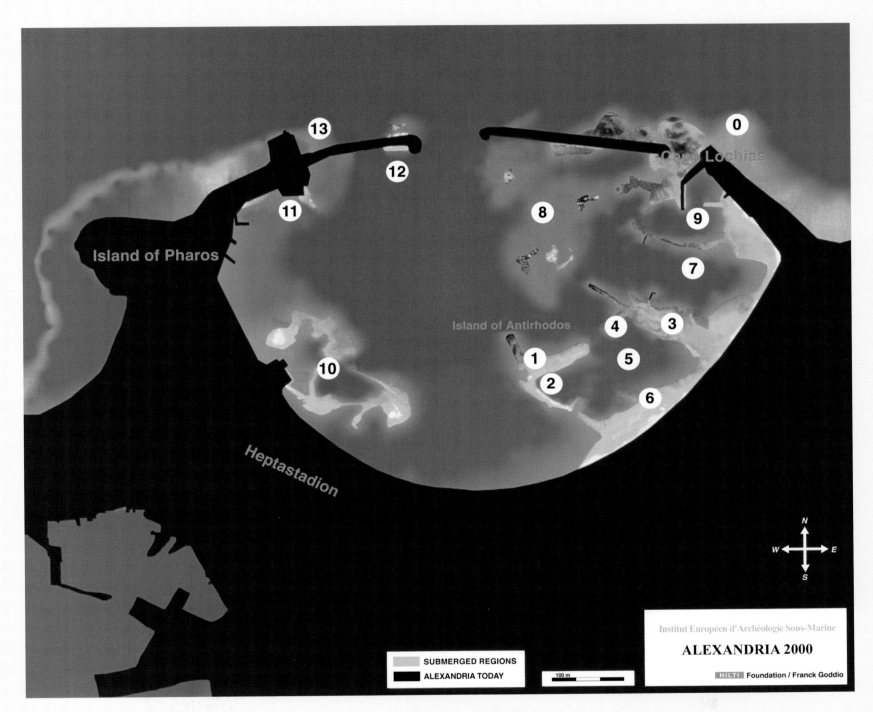

SUBMERGED REGIONS
ALEXANDRIA TODAY

100 m

Institut Européen d'Archéologie Sous-Marine

ALEXANDRIA 2000

HILTI Foundation / Franck Goddio

0. Cape Lochias
1. island of Antirhodos
2. small private harbour on the island of Antirhodos
3. Poseidium
4. Timonium
5. third harbour
6. ancient coastline
7. second large harbour
8. reefs
9. inner harbour
10. harbour basins
11. moles and docks on the island of Pharos
12. large reefs with remains of limestone constructions
13. jumble of architectural remains from different periods.

The film crew preparing to dive in Alexandria's eastern harbour.

Moulding the past

Georges Brocot, an archaeologist and specialist in archaeological casting, is the man on board responsible for this part of the operation. He explains: "Thanks to the technique of casting, the international experts who follow our missions can have immediate access to the archaeological material and study it in different locations round the world simultaneously. I always work on board the base ship, alongside the divers, so that I am on the spot when any new discovery is made."

At Alexandria we generally use two techniques of casting: stamping – taking a surface impression, either under the water or at the surface; and three-dimensional casting, which involves making a mould. Both techniques produce results true to the original.

At the request of the Egyptian authorities Brocot cast two magnificent statues using 3-D moulds, which were shown at an exhibition at the UN's headquarters in New York.

Stamping

This technique is generally used for huge blocks of stone on which inscriptions have been engraved. The divers begin by carefully cleaning the blocks with scrapers and small burins. Meanwhile, colleagues working on the surface place a layer of silicone on to a durable and flexible fabric, varying the thickness according to the depth of the motifs on the surface of the block. The divers then attach this fabric coating to the surface of the inscription and cover it with a sheet of lead, which they hammer gently to ensure that the silicone moulds into the smallest crevices of the inscription. Finally it is all fastened down to provide better protection against the movement of the sea.

The silicone layer is removed from the mould between 16 and 24 hours later, once polymerisation (the transformation of the silicone into a flexible membrane) has taken place.

The inscription then appears in reverse on the membrane and sometimes it is possible to read inscriptions that were illegible or invisible on the seabed. The silicone makes it

Georges Brocot,
moulding specialist

Taking a silicone impression underwater

A sheet of material impregnated with silicone, the same size as the block to be stamped, is lowered into the sea and floated down to the bottom

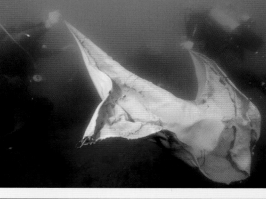

The material is placed on top of the block and covered with sheets of lead.

The sheets are gently hammered so that the material adheres closely to the surface of the block, achieving perfect contact with the incised forms.

The lead sheets are strapped in place so that constant pressure can be maintained during the process of polymerisation.

Eighteen hours later, the mould is withdrawn. The silicone has polymerised and the stamp is complete.

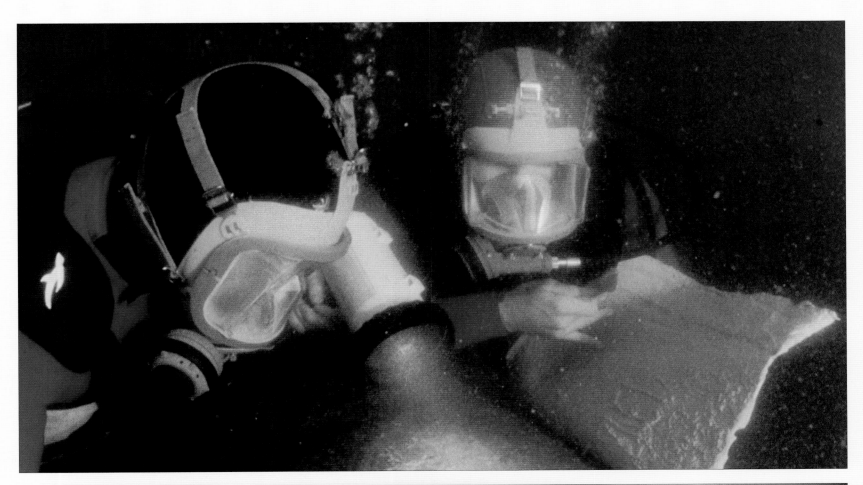

Taking an impression of a fragment from an obelisk. The process of stamping on a silicone membrane enables archaeologists to study it in the minutest detail. The impression also reveals tool marks, which demonstrate the skill of the ancient craftsmen.

possible to obtain details with remarkable accuracy, down to a micron (1/1000mm). On board the *Princess Duda* the membrane is photographed in oblique light using a digital camera. The image can be studied straightaway on the computer screen, then e-mailed to the epigraphers and other international experts.

Stamping can also be done at the surface if the blocks of stone are not too large to be raised by crane. The process is similar, though not identical, to the underwater procedure.

After the inscription has been cleaned and rinsed in fresh water, it is then covered in a solution of polyvinyl alcohol, which forms a colourless plastic, water-soluble film which aids the process of removing the membrane.

Several successive layers of silicone, to a depth of 5 or 6mm, are then cast (without using material). No lead sheet or strapping is necessary, and the result is a supple and clearly legible membrane.

Right: André and Étienne Bernand, experienced epigraphers, read the impressions of Greek inscriptions taken from the bases of statues discovered on the island of Antirhodos.

Below: two blocks of granite discovered more than 500m apart were brought together and a stamp was taken, which showed that the two blocks originally formed a single piece. We can see from the stamp that one of the fragments was more eroded than the other: the inscriptions on the left of the picture (belonging to the block found near the coast) are more faint than those on the other fragment which was discovered on the island of Antirhodos.

Hieroglyphs 'stamped' on a sheet of silicone. These ones are extremely ancient: the Ptolemies, the last of Egypt's pharaohs, had a habit of embellishing their palaces with architectural elements, transported from Upper Egypt, that were already regarded as antiquities in their own time. The end of this inscription, discovered on the island of Antirhodos, reads: "[The king] … living eternally".

Making a mould

Once it had been raised to the surface, the statue of the priest holding the Canopic vase was mechanically cleaned using microburins and scalpels. This is the moment when the specialist needs to analyse the complexity of the piece, its size, shape, weight, etc.

Because of the cramped and unstable conditions on board it was important to choose a quick and simple method. So I decided to mould the statues in two halves. I commenced by masking the microfissures in the stone prior to determining where to position the join between the two halves of the mould (which will come together to form the statue) and the vents through which the resin would flow to fill the mould. The statue was then half submerged in a perfectly level bed of plastiline (a sort of modelling clay), which served as a base for the construction of the first half-mould. Then at least two or three layers of extremely fluid silicone were cast in order to ensure perfect definition, before the addition of further layers of a thicker consistency, bringing the total thickness to between 8 and 10mm. Once polymerisation had occurred, I made a casing (a hard shell of epoxy resin) to cover the silicone

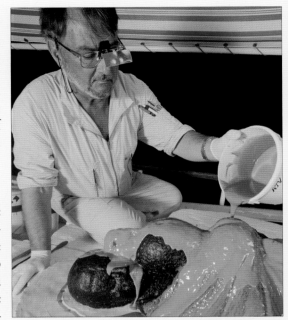

membrane. This combination of membrane and outer shell is designed to recreate the exact form of the statue at the moment of casting.

The bed of plastiline is then removed, and the statue is turned over along with the first half of the mould. The second half of the mould will then be made using the same method.

Casting

Back in my workshop in France, at the request of the Egyptian authorities, I produced a cast for the UN exhibition. The way I do this is by pouring epoxy resin into the mould or on to the membrane of an impression. This resin is dyed to match the colour of the original archaeological material and allowed to harden for 48 hours. Once the casting has been stripped, all that I have to do is to restore minute details by applying a patina with paint brushes and an airbrush (a small paint gun allowing highly precise application), in order to achieve a true copy.

Georges (right) pouring silicone over the statue of the priest, ensuring that the entire piece is evenly covered. Acupuncture needles (below) are used to control the thickness of the material, and the whole thing is then covered with a rigid shell of epoxy resin.

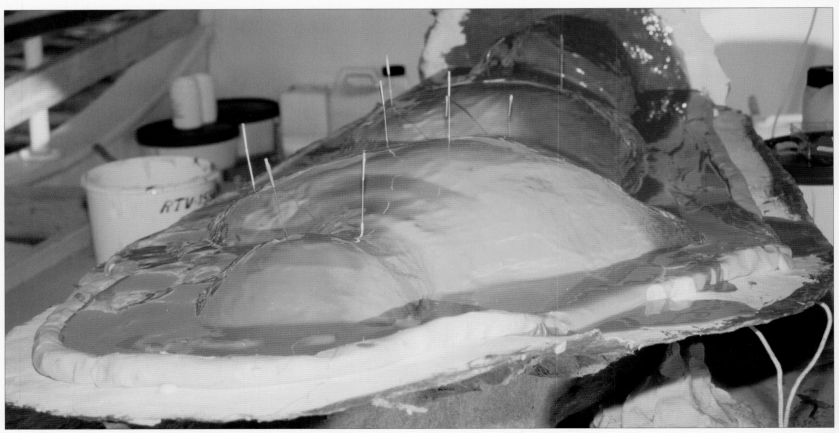

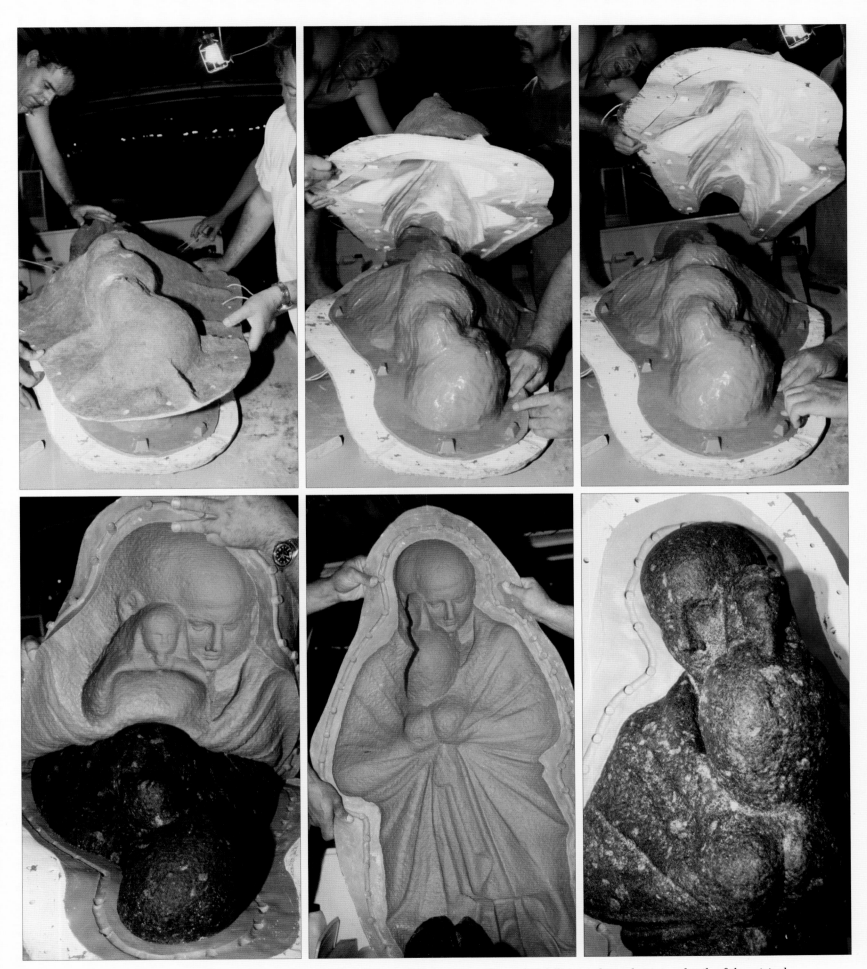

An emotional moment: the mould being lifted from the statue of the priest. The silicone membrane faithfully reproduces the tiniest details of the original.

A mould being made of the sphinx representing Ptolemy XII.

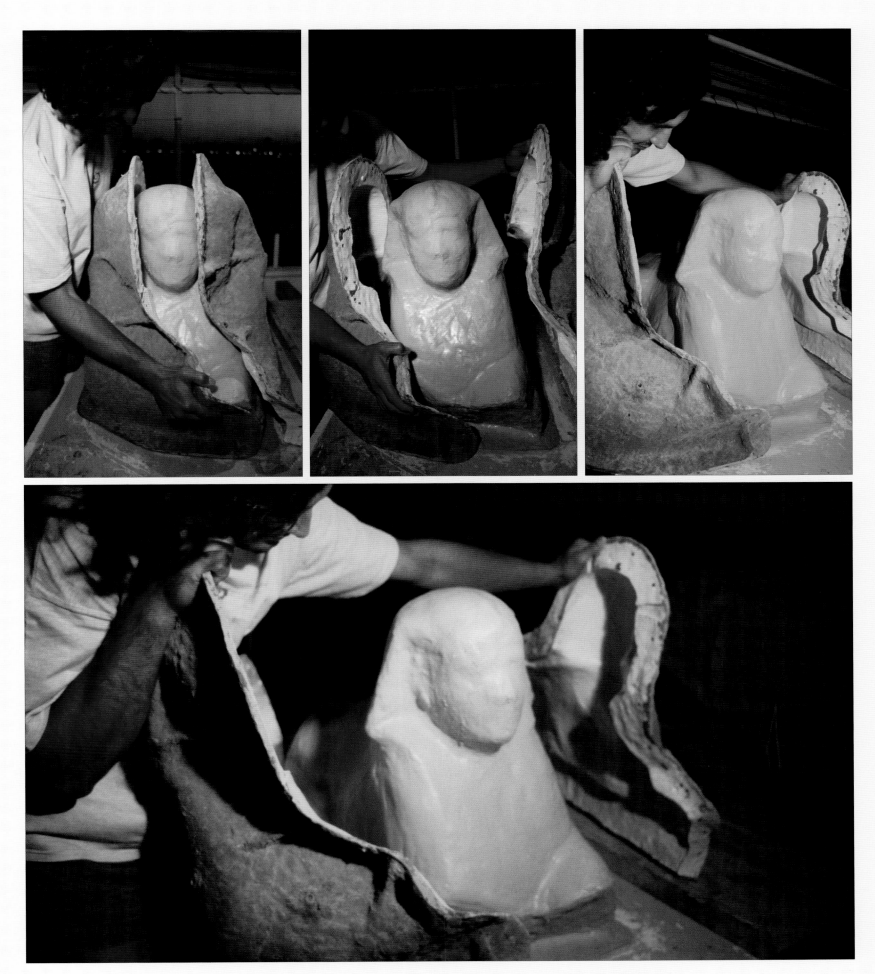

Once the statue of the sphinx is removed from the mould, the two parts of the 3-D mould are then reassembled and bolted together.

Underwater photography

**Christoph Gerigk,
photographer**

"Taking successful underwater shots at Alexandria is a real technical challenge, since conventional rules of photography do not apply," says Christoph Gerigk, a photographer with the Goddio expeditions, whose underwater images regularly appear in major international magazines. For his work in Egypt Christoph has even been awarded two prizes by World Press Photo, a prestigious competition which annually rewards the best press photographers world-wide.

"Being a German by birth, I am used to the bad diving conditions in the North Sea; but the reduced visibility – often less than a metre – in the harbour at Alexandria still came as a surprise, reminding me in some strange way of the flooded gravel pits where I learnt to dive. On the other hand, the colour and density of the particles suspended in the water change from hour to hour, depending on the currents and also on the pollution and the development of micro-organisms. The water can change from bright blue to green, to yellow, red, maroon and black… It is visibility, in short, that determines which archaeological objects I photograph and consequently the maximum distance possible between the subject and the camera (either general view or close up)."

Christoph works under constant pressure, as he must take the best photographs he can when the water is at its clearest. This is why he generally uses 18mm wide-angle lenses, which offer a 100° diagonal angle of view that allows him to get as close as possible to his subject without distorting the image. "My lenses are mounted on Nikon reflex cameras, enclosed in Seacam water-

General view, taken in 1998, showing the statue of the priest carrying a Canopic vase. It took no fewer than five days to set the scene for this photograph – to find the right angles of view and arrange the lighting so that it enhanced the sense of mystery and showed off the statues and columns to best effect. It was thanks to exceptionally good visibility that everything came together in the end.

tight cases made of metal alloy that are specially designed to resist the aggressive effects of pollution. The cameras are linked to powerful electronic flash lights, mounted on long articulated arms or triggered at a distance by cables and photocells. Adjusting the artificial lighting for the flash is a real headache, since the water diffuses the light differently depending on its colour! On top of that, the films (professional 100 ASAs) have to be developed with reference to the light conditions so that the right kind of contrast can be achieved. As a precaution I always take a great many photographs of archaeological objects in different lighting conditions."

Christoph often dives with four or five photographic cases, two Nikonos (underwater cameras) and six flash lights, which he hooks on to himself, and it is not always easy to handle so much equipment when there is also a swell to contend with. "I go down with the divers when they are working and recovering new finds. It is the divers in my opinion who provide the human dimension to the adventure," says Christoph, whose ultimate aim is to transmit to the spectator something of the emotion, and the mystery, that attends each new discovery.

Christoph's job is also to photograph the objects on their own, producing the sort of documentary images that appear in scientific publications as part of the concluding chapter of any archaeological mission. "I very much like working in the gloom," he says, "because it helps to create an atmosphere of mystery and show certain objects to advantage. My best memory is of a general view, taken in 1998 and showing fragments of statues among fallen columns. It took me five days to find some good angles of view, set up flash lights all over the place (while staying out of the shot myself) and hide the cables in the sand. In the course of successive dives visibility became exceptionally good (5m) and enabled me to produce a number of truly unexpected documentary images."

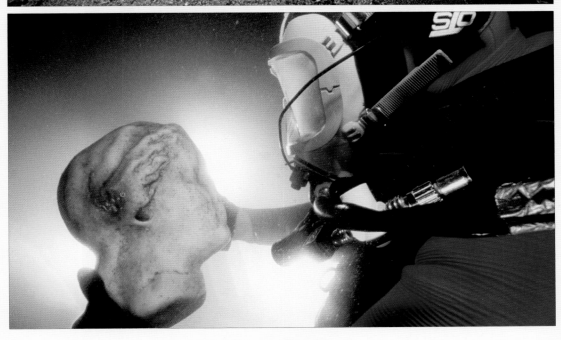

The ibis was sacred to the god Thoth-Hermes. Although its head is missing, this one still gives us an idea of the sculpture's original elegance. The bird's long thin neck and pointed beak posed a problem when it came to sculpting them in stone; the missing head would in fact have been made out of metal and later attached to the body.

Making documentary films for television

"Making a documentary film in the disgustingly filthy waters of Alexandria harbour is something of a challenge!" says Roland Savoye, cameraman and co-producer of the Goddio team's television documentaries, who has been coming to the Bay of Alexandria every year since 1995 to film the divers' latest discoveries. Roland has had years of experience working in the worlds of advertising and film production and is responsible for the aquatic and underwater scenes in *Astérix et Obélix: Mission Cléopâtre* by Alain Chabat, *Est-Ouest* by Régis Wargnier, *Ridicule* and *La Fille sur le Pont* by Patrice Leconte, and *La*

**Roland Savoye,
producer of underwater films**

Cité des Enfants Perdus by Caro and Jeunet. "Today," he goes on, "in the harbour at Alexandria, visibility is so poor (0–4m) that I am forced to work incredibly fast, always watching out for the smallest sign of clearer water. I feel as if I have to steal each

image I succeed in shooting underwater! "I use a Betacam SP video camera equipped with an optical system adapted to underwater conditions. The camera is enclosed in a Cinémarine watertight housing and has a video viewfinder and external controls. Down at the bottom my two assistants, Pascal Morisset and John Rogers, swoop about like acrobats lighting the sequences using powerful HMI lamps. These lamps are designed to reproduce daylight and can penetrate very effectively in water. Pascal and John angle the light at 45° in order to avoid reflection from suspended particles, or alternatively shine it from above – a technique that we call

Roland Savoye and his assistants dive to the bottom to film the team's final discoveries. Time is of the essence – if conditions deteriorate, it may be impossible to take any more shots between now and the end of the mission. Here they are seen filming a diorite head from the Saitic period, discovered at the Canopus-East site.

'showering'. The effects can be really surprising. My aim is to transform the cloudy water into something harmoniously soft-focus that increases a natural sense of mystery. I am also constantly trying to convey the emotion surrounding each discovery – with the help, that is, of the divers.

"Before each dive I repeat the sequences with them, regulating every little movement and gesture: a hand trembling with excitement as it touches the face of a statue, an expression of surprise as some Greek inscriptions emerge from layers of deposits, or as the camera pans over a majestic vista of ancient columns... It is up to the divers to convey the emotion and the dreamy atmosphere of each discovery. But the fish that swim into the camera's field of view also remind us – because it is sometimes easy to forget – that all this is happening underwater.

"Out of all my time spent filming in the bay, one marvellous memory stands out: the moment when the statue of the priest with the Canopic vase was raised up from the bottom. There was a crowd of journalists waiting at the surface and it all happened very fast. I had to capture the spirit and emotion of that moment in a single shot while we were swimming up to the surface! It was the last shot I took of the priest under the sea. One other such moment had me glued behind my viewfinder, watching in fascination as an extraordinary gold ring, surmounted by an intaglio representing a bird, suddenly emerged out of the pitch darkness where the divers were manoeuvring...

"Besides underwater shots I also shoot scenes on board the *Princess Duda*, to show what the life of the team is really like, whether we are talking about the excitement of discovering new finds, or the difficulties of working under water in poor visibility, or the exhaustion experienced by the divers, or whatever. These lived scenes have been integrated into a documentary film lasting 52 minutes and entitled *Alexandrie: La Cité Engloutie*, which has been broadcast on Canal Plus and France 5 as well as on a number of European channels. An American version, *Cleopatra's Palace*, has also been well received on Discovery Channel's world-wide network."

The statue of the priest being filmed as it is hoisted to the surface.

Shots taken on board the support vessel. Small artefacts are photographed inside this black box.

Restoration and conservation of the archaeological material

"The way to date an archaeological site with accuracy is to study the pottery. Pottery remains are often the first objects that can be dated and they tell us a great deal about the tastes, culinary habits and trading channels of the time," says Catherine Grataloup, an archaeologist specialising in the study of pottery. "Excavations in Alexandria harbour have recovered pottery that is remarkably well preserved: many of the pieces are still intact and easily identifiable. This is a clear advantage compared with terrestrial sites, where (with the exception of certain specific sites such as burial grounds) we are only likely to find fragments…

"Once the underwater sediments have been cleaned off, we look carefully at the shape, texture and decoration of the pottery so that we can determine its date and provenance. Excavations at Alexandria have unearthed pieces dating from the 3rd century BC to the 4th century AD. Some of them have been recovered in large quantities and are described as 'common'. These everyday items – drinking cups, cooking pots, pitchers, oil lamps, plates, wine amphorae, etc. – were produced in Alexandria itself (as we can ascertain from

the clay), but imported pottery, termed 'fine' and sometimes decorated, has also been found, as well as amphorae from Greece, Cyprus and North Africa.

"After it has been identified, each object, whether it is a complete piece or just a sherd, is described, measured, numbered and photographed, before being drawn using a conformator (an instrument equipped with thin, mobile lamellas used to draw the outline of the object) and a slide square (a tool for measuring the thickness of the material). All this information is then fed into a database, which provides an ideal means of carrying out statistical studies or locating the archaeological material on the site plan…

"As well as being studied, the pottery is mechanically cleaned using microburins and scalpels to remove any deposits and shells," continues Olivier Berger, an archaeologist, chemist and specialist in the conservation and restoration of underwater archaeological material. "It is then immersed in fresh water so that the salts contained in the fired clay can be removed by osmosis. This stage is controlled by taking measurements of electric conductivity while the pieces are soaking in the basins. Following desalination, the pottery

is restored. Fragments are glued together and, where necessary, gaps are filled in and a tint is applied. Pieces that have been lightly fired and therefore fragile are consolidated with a resin. The pottery is then stored in a room where the temperature and humidity are kept at a constant level to prevent salts re-forming on its surface and to maintain its condition for possible display purposes. "The process is more or less the same for statues and other architectural objects made of stone. Marble, limestone and sandstone, however, require a longer desalination time than basalt or granite, which are less permeable. Objects which break up are consolidated with a 'reversible' acrylic resin, and fragments of statues are reassembled by dowelling.

"Organic archaeological material (wood, leather, bone, etc.) requires swift and delicate treatment as soon as it has been recovered. After cleaning and desalination, the waterlogged material is dried out slowly and systematically and the excess water is gradually replaced with a resin so that the volume of the material is maintained.

"Metals require equally complex restoration and conservation measures. Although gold (being the noble metal *par excellence*)

Ceramic jar found in Alexandria's eastern harbour.

remains completely unaltered, bronze, silver, iron and lead, on the other hand, immediately corrode on exposure to the air. Once the deposits have been removed, objects made of these metals are immersed in a desalination bath equipped with a regulated and precise system of chemical or electrochemical treatment. Following elimination of the salts, the material is restored (chemically and ultrasonically) and its original surface is revived. It is then chemically stabilised in order to halt the process of corrosion prior to being covered with a varnish and a wax which protect it from moisture in the air. It is stored at a constant temperature and humidity to prevent any corrosion re-occurring."

Oil lamp discovered in Alexandria's eastern harbour.

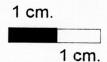

1 cm.

1 cm.

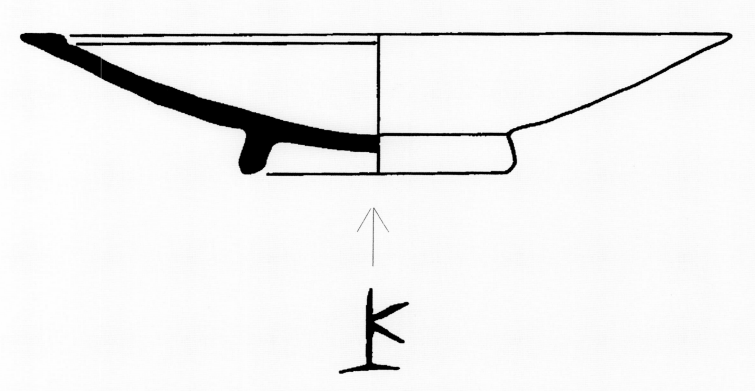

A ceramic dish found in the royal port, off the island of Antirhodos, drawn by Mahat Ezz el Din.

Ceramic vessels discovered in Antirhodos' royal port

PART TWO

The Portus Magnus of Alexandria

Mareotis lake
and river harbour

Hippodamian
town plan

Royal Emporium

3rd port

Timonium

2nd port

Breakwater

1st port

Large central
reef

Natural reefs

Cape Lochias

S

E — W

Prevailing wind

N

Canal

Kibotos

Heptastadion

Island of
Antirhodos

Port
Public emporium

Main fairway

Fairway

Lighthouse

Island of Pharos

Outlying reefs

Ancient Alexandria

Imaginary 3-D reconstruction of the site at Alexandria, based on the real topographical data collected by the IEASM.
The locations of the Heptastadion, the lighthouse and the Kibotos are hypothetical.

*Computer-generated view of Alexandria's Portus Magnus based on the findings of the IEASM,
in collaboration with Egypt's Supreme Council for Antiquities
Graphics: Yann Bernard
Copyright: Franck Goddio/Hilti Foundation*

The royal quarters

In Ptolemaic times, any navigator who entered the roads at Alexandria, after successfully negotiating the outlying reefs, was met with the following panorama: not a single harbour and a single palace, but a promontory covered with royal residences, princely dwellings, temples and several harbours. The traveller curious about such marvels today is obliged to leap from his boat and dive, not merely beneath the waters of the bay, but also back in time — as we did, armed with oxygen cylinders and galvanised by stories from the past.

Sections of paving, like this one, dating back to the time of the Ptolemies, have been found along the entire length of the ancient coastline.

*I*f you wish to enjoy an unblemished youth, you must found a glorious city. So spoke the oracle who inspired Alexander the Great to found the equally great city that bears his name. 'Great' is the epithet that appears most frequently in the written texts, after 'beautiful', 'eternal', 'royal' and 'brilliant'. Alexander's dream was to found a gigantic city, and following his death (in 323 BC) that city continued to grow. At the time of the Romans it is estimated that it could accommodate a population of some 500,000 inhabitants.

As the site of the royal residence, Alexandria benefited from the Ptolemaic rulers' penchant for luxury, since successive rulers had a habit of constructing new and ever more magnificent palaces to supplement the existing buildings. The royal courtesans were housed in neighbouring residences and they too demonstrated a passion for ornament and ostentation. It was not just a handful of buildings that could be described as royal, but an entire district.

The Greek geographer and historian Strabo, who visited Alexandria between 27 and 20 BC, describes it in the following terms: *The city has some splendid gardens and also houses the royal buildings, which occupy a quarter or even a third of the total area, since each of the kings, being anxious to embellish the public buildings with some new ornamentation of his own, was no less eager to add a new residence to the existing ones at his own expense. We can now say of them, in the words of the poet, therefore, that they "are born one from another". All these buildings form a continuous construction, together with the port and even those buildings which extend beyond the port.*

From dream to reality

The majority of Alexandria's royal quarters were destroyed and submerged as a result of massive subsidence along its coastline. Today we are in a position to prove that, in the course of the last 2,000 years, the sea level at Alexandria has risen by 1–1.5m and the ground level has fallen by 5–6m. When we first approached the site, the only maps that we had at our disposal depended upon interpretations of the ancient texts. We were familiar, of course, with these extraordinary descriptions, but we made a decision not to refer to them again until we had succeeded in recreating the map of this lost world on the basis of real surveys relying exclusively on observations carried out on site.

We began by producing maps using electronic instruments: magnetic maps, maps locating notable points detected by side scan sonar, bathymetric maps and

Wooden post supporting a heap of limestone blocks, discovered after clearing away sediment. Parallel rows of similar piles and stones were used to reinforce the foundations of the moles situated in the western part of the Portus Magnus.

finally geological maps indicating the different sedimentary strata and the scars caused by natural disasters. The areas that showed anomalies were excavated to enable visual identification of the structures. The survey maps were then compared with the maps showing recovered remains, and gradually the 'true' shores of the lost Alexandria began to emerge.

After more than 11,000 diving hours, we were in a position to draw up a map of the royal quarters – and demonstrate that the 1886 map based on the texts, the map which had previously been the only authority, was in fact totally flawed. The new configuration was more logical. The long breakwater, for example, at the end of which the Timonium had been drawn could not possibly have been so exposed: such a construction would not have lasted more than a single winter. And here was the island of Antirhodos suddenly assuming a new shape and a different position, justifying the description of its small harbour as 'perfect'.

It was only then that we reread Strabo and the other ancient authors: everything coincided and the pieces of the puzzle began to fit together.

Tour of the horizon

Alexandria is built on a strip of coastline separating the Mediterranean from Lake Maerotis, west of the Nile Delta. The roadstead is very exposed to the sea winds and is closed in by a number of reefs and two headlands: Cape Lochias and the island of Pharos, an ancient island connected to the mainland by a mole, the Heptastadion, which was constructed at the behest of Ptolemy Soter (322–283 BC). This addition created two harbours: to the east, the Great Port (Portus Magnus), which has been the object of archaeological excavation, and the Eunostos, now encompassed within the site of the current commercial port.

The current roadstead is protected by two breakwaters, built in the 20th century, probably on the site of existing remains, which thereby became inaccessible. A great mole was built in the Ptolemaic era, probably where the eastern breakwater now stands, and served to protect the harbour against the swell caused by the northerly winds. Several authors mention the danger posed by the scattered reefs: only the central channel or 'main fairway' permitted relatively risk-free access to the harbour, although two other small fairways are also mentioned.

The excavated area, the Portus Magnus, can be divided into five large sectors: Cape Lochias, the ancient coastline, the Poseidium peninsula, the island of Antirhodos and the western harbour installations. In these five sectors, wherever paving is still present, the surfaces prove to be smooth, implying that the town planners undertook a project of levelling or raising the original rocky terrain. Over the 600 hectares surveyed, thousands of artefacts have been discovered and cleaned of their limestone deposits, layers that are sometimes as much as 60cm thick. All that remained once these objects had been cleaned was to identify them and, if possible, deduce what function they once fulfilled.

These large limestone slabs give us an idea of the dimensions of the original esplanade, which was clearly capable of supporting buildings of substantial size.

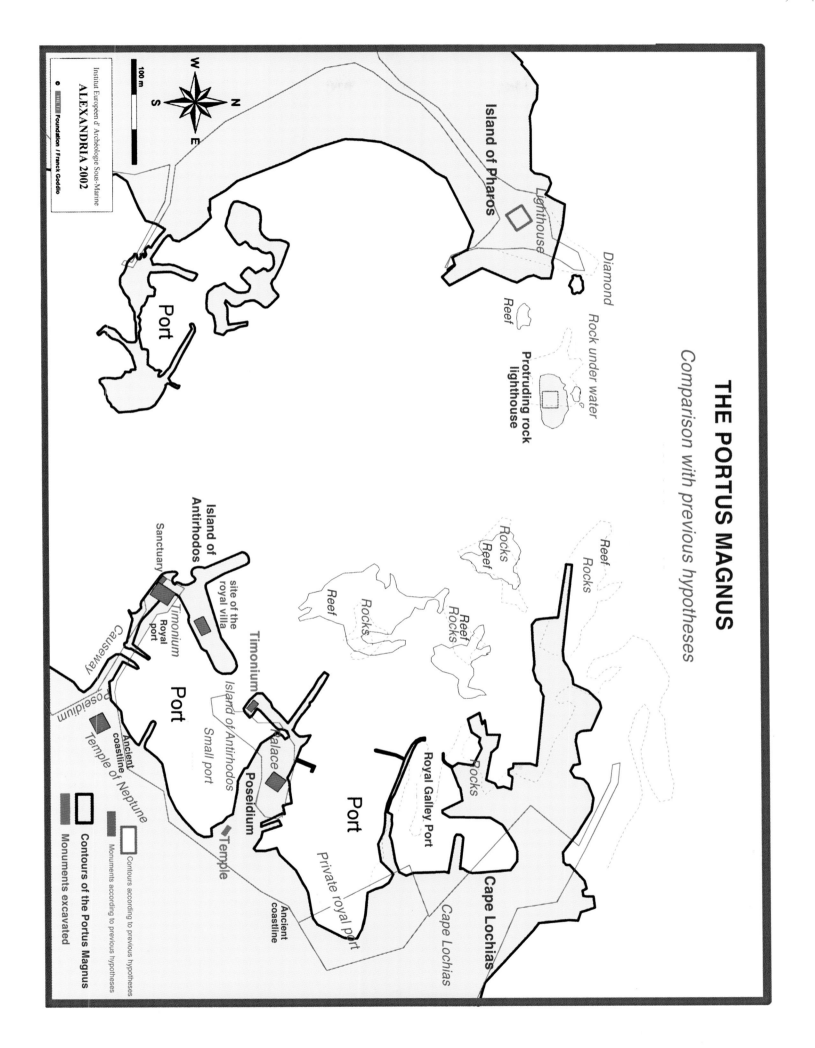

THE PORTUS MAGNUS

Comparison with previous hypotheses

Island of Pharos

Lighthouse

Diamond
Reef

Rock under water

Protruding rock
lighthouse

Port

Sanctuary

Island of
Antirhodos

Timonium
Royal
port

site of the
royal villa

Causeway

Poseidium

Timonium

Island of Antirhodos

Small port

Palace

Poseidium

Temple

Port

Ancient
coastline

Temple of Neptune

Port

Private royal port

Reef
Rocks

Rocks
Reef

Reef

Rocks

Reef
Rocks

Rocks

Royal Galley Port

Cape Lochias

Cape Lochias

Ancient
coastline

Rocks

Contours of the Portus Magnus

Contours according to previous hypotheses

Monuments excavated

Monuments according to previous hypotheses

Institut Européen d'Archéologie Sous-Marine
ALEXANDRIA 2002

Foundation / Franck Goddio

100 m

N W S E

77

Above: the head of a Roman princess, mother of the Emperor Claudius, lying on the sea-bed at Alexandria – a moving association of two different cultures. Below: Hermes' knee. Examination of sculptural details can reveal the influence of more than one culture in a single piece of statuary.

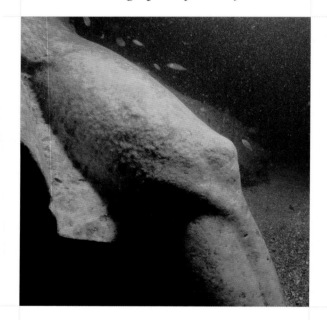

The mystery of the pharaonica

What is Alexandria's greatest mystery? Cleopatra's nose? The burning of the great library? Perhaps the most intriguing question regarding this lost civilisation, in fact, is how the two cultures, Greek and Egyptian, were able to co-exist there. Should we even be speaking of co-existence, or rather of merging, interaction, mutual absorption? Was there conflict or symbiosis between the Hellenistic and the Pharaonic cultures? Where was Alexandria, in short? Was it a kind of overseas territory belonging to Greece or a mutant cell that was nevertheless part of the body of Egypt? Professor Jean Yoyotte proposed the term 'pharaonica' to describe the remains that have been discovered at this cultural crossroads: neither aegyptiaca, nor hellenica, but monuments of Hellenic culture conceived in the time of the Pharaohs.

As supreme commander of the Greeks and their allies, Alexander founded a city that was indisputably Greek: the architects who designed it were Greek, Greek was spoken there, the name of the place and of its inhabitants was Greek, and the temples were dedicated to Zeus, Poseidon and other Olympian gods. Moreover, Alexandria was not said to be in Egypt, but 'on the edge of Egypt' (*ad Aegyptum*), and the distinction was significant. And yet the city was quick to adopt as its patron the Memphian god Osiris-Apis, under the name Serapis, and housed a number of sanctuaries dedicated to the sorceress Isis, who was to enjoy increasing popularity with the Greek and later Roman population. In the 1st and 2nd centuries BC the patron of Alexandria was frequently invoked by the name of Zeus-Helios-Serapis, an extraordinary fusion which henceforth assumed the character of a universal sun god. Numerous strictly Egyptian remains discovered at Alexandria were imported from Heliopolis, a very ancient city situated to the north-west of Cairo and dedicated, as its name suggests, to the cult of Ra, god of the sun (*Helios* in Greek).

The study of sculptures and architectural ornaments discovered in Alexandria's royal quarters produces some intriguing answers, or rather raises further questions that are even more intriguing regarding the conditions of this mixed marriage. The two architectural traditions were opposed from the outset. Egyptian temples were closed, Greek temples open. There were also radical differences in terms of organisation and style of imagery. And yet, although it would be wrong to talk of fusion, iconographic exchanges were operating between the two cultures. Egyptian gods were featured draped in costumes that were typically Greek. Heracles, the Greek hero par excellence, known as Khonsu in the country of the Nile, is depicted, with his club, in a graphic style that is pure Egyptian, while the sphinx, though remaining an intrinsically Egyptian representation, assumed Hellenistic facial characteristics and headdresses. The sacred area of Egyptian temples was enclosed by a high wall in front of which stood pairs of colossi. The Ptolemies and the Caesars embraced this hieratic iconography and erected gigantic statues exaggerating the superhuman nature of their divinity. The stiff posture, bearing, stylised musculature, royal clothes and crowns are in the pure Pharaonic tradition, but the curly hair hanging below the *nemes* (Egyptian royal headdress) is resolutely Greek.

The messenger of the gods, known to the Greeks as Hermes and to the Egyptians as Thoth, is identified here by his cloak, pinned back on his right shoulder – a typically Hellenistic feature, later adopted by the Romans.

Exoticism at home

There does not appear to have been an organised indigenous religious cult at Alexandria. What was the reason therefore for the existence of so many ornamental elements of Egyptian origin? It is particularly difficult to trace the history of these objects: displaced, either individually or en masse, re-used for purposes that were either utilitarian (for which they were sometimes refashioned) or ideological, in accordance or otherwise with their primary significance, victims of mutilation, either natural or iconoclastic, such objects are surrounded with uncertainty.

One possible explanation for this abundance of imports is as follows. The Egyptian objects may have been re-used in the Greek temples initially in an ornamental capacity and then later subsumed into religious practice (let us not forget that Isis had given rise to a cult that was organised *à la Grecque*). In the Greek city of Alexandria, ancient Egypt may thus have provided an element of exoticism. Not immediately, it is true – Ptolemaic Alexandria would initially have been a Greek world 'alongside Egypt' and the introduction of ancient Egypt would only have occurred at a later date, under the influence of a Graeco-Roman 'Egyptomania'. A detailed study of aesthetic currents manifesting themselves through the submerged artefacts gave us the perfect opportunity to test this theory.

The badly eroded head of a sphinx. Identification can be problematic in such cases.

This Greek inscription – one of the treasures that such blocks can conceal – only came to light after the surface of the stone had been cleaned. Specialists will examine a stamped impression taken using a silicone membrane.

"Let us stay face to face, your hands in mine / While beneath the bridge of our arms / the weary wave of eternal glances flows / Let night come and the hour sound / Days pass; I stay."
Guillaume Apollinaire, "Le pont Mirabeau", Alcools.

The Ptolemies

Coin representing Ptolemy I Soter and Queen Berenice I.
© The American Numismatic Society

Coin representing Ptolemy II Philadelphus and Queen Arsinoë II.
© The American Numismatic Society

The Ptolemies' family tree (p. 86) offers plenty of scope for those who are interested in deciphering the meaning and derivation of names.

It is important to warn the reader at this point, however, that the dates attributed to these kings and queens are an invention of modern historians and not classical usage. It is also worth mentioning that the term 'Lagid' (descendants of Lagos), which is also often used to refer to the Ptolemies, was not used in antiquity. The name derives from Alexander's general, Lagos, who founded the dynasty and signifies not 'hare' (*lagos*) – which would be somewhat surprising in the case of a general – but 'leader of the people' (*agon* and *laos*), a name which clearly confers greater status.

These linguistic pitfalls are nothing compared to the choice of names applied to the dynastic rulers. If we take a close look at their family tree we see that three sorts of epithets were applied to the Ptolemies. A first group, including Ptolemy I, Ptolemy III and Ptolemy V, comprises names emphasising the competence of these kings: Soter signifies 'saviour', Euergetes 'doer of good deeds' and Epiphanes 'who manifests himself'. A second group, comprising Ptolemy II, Ptolemy IV and Ptolemy VI, brings together kings bearing qualifiers with a family reference: Philadelphus 'who loves his sister', Philopator 'who loves his father' and Philometor 'who loves his mother'.

A third group includes names implying the reincarnation of former kings in the person of their successors. So we have Ptolemy VII Neos Philopator, Ptolemy VIII Euergetes II, Ptolemy IX Soter II, Ptolemy X Alexander I and Theos Philometor, Ptolemy XII Alexander II, while one title – Ptolemy XII Theos Dionysus – implies divine incarnation.

A number of the Ptolemies were also given nicknames by their subjects and these were a great deal less flattering than the official names. Ptolemy VII Euergetes II was nicknamed Phykston, 'ball of fat'; Ptolemy IX Soter received the nickname Lathyrus or 'chickpea'; and Ptolemy XII Neos Dionysus was also known, less offensively, as Auletes or 'flute player'. The last of the Ptolemies, Cleopatra VII – and the women of the dynasty in general – escaped these popular sobriquets.

The family tree demonstrates the Egyptian practice of intermarriage within the royal family, a practice which was not in fact adopted from the outset. Ptolemy I, son of Lagos, followed the example of Alexander the Great: despite the fact that he had no real penchant for women, he nevertheless married a Persian by the name of Apama (according to Plutarch), or Arkama (according to Arrian), who was the daughter of Artabazos. He later married Eurydice, daughter of Antipatros, who left Egypt in 287 BC. His next wife, Berenice I, daughter of Magas, gave birth to the future Ptolemy II Philadelphus. This Ptolemy was the first to intermarry, uniting himself with his sister Arsinoë following an earlier marriage to Arsinoë I, daughter of Lysimachus of Thrace. Ptolemy III Euergetes I did not marry his sister Berenice, who was already married to Antiochus II, king of Syria, and was assassinated at Daphnae. He married Berenice I, daughter of Magas of Cyrene, who was assassinated by her son, Ptolemy IV Philopator. The latter married his younger sister Arsinoë III, who was assassinated by the king's mistress. This couple only had one child, Ptolemy V Epiphanes, who, having no sister, married Cleopatra I, daughter of Antiochus III of Syria. Three children were born of this union and each occupied the throne of Egypt in turn: Ptolemy VI Philometor, Ptolemy VIII Euergetes II and Cleopatra III.

All future royal marriages were made within the reigning family. Cleopatra II married first her older brother Ptolemy VI Philometor, then her second brother Ptolemy VIII Euergetes II. The fourth child of Ptolemy VI Philometor and Cleopatra II would have reigned as Ptolemy VII Neos Philopator, but he was assassinated by his uncle Ptolemy VIII Euergetes II and so does not figure in the genealogy. Ptolemy VIII Euergetes II later married his niece Cleopatra III.

Ptolemy IX Soter II, son of Ptolemy VIII Euergetes II and Cleopatra III, intermarried twice, marrying first his sister Cleopatra IV, then his other sister Cleopatra Selene, 'Moon', who later married

Antiochus VIII Grippos, then Antiochus IX Kyzitiemos and Antiochus X Enseber Philopator, before being assassinated at Seleucia on the Euphrates.

The non-consanguineous and non-dynastic marriage contracted by Ptolemy IX Soter II with an unknown woman is an event of great significance in the evolution of the dynasty. This woman gave him four children: Ptolemy, later king of Cyprus; Ptolemy XII Neos Dionysus Auletes, who became king of Egypt; Cleopatra V Tryphaina, and perhaps one other daughter named Cleopatra VI Tryphanea.

Ptolemy X Alexander I, son of Ptolemy VIII and Cleopatra III (uncle and niece), had a son by an unknown woman. This was Ptolemy XI Alexander II, who married his cousin Berenice III and held power for only a matter of weeks before being assassinated.

The great Cleopatra (Cleopatra VII) had a son by Julius Caesar, Caesarion, whose title was Ptolemy XV Caesar Philopator Philometor. Caesarion was co-regent with his mother from 44 to 30 BC and was assassinated on the orders of Octavian.

Cleopatra and Mark Antony had a son named Alexander Helios, 'Sun', who was proclaimed king of Armenia, Media and the country of the Parthians, and of all the other countries that lay between the Euphrates and the Indus. Alexander Helios married Jatapa of Media. His twin sister, Cleopatra Selene, 'Moon', married Juba of Mauritania. Mark Antony and Cleopatra had one other child, a son named Ptolemy Philadelphus. All three of their children were taken to Rome by Octavian.

It would be too time-consuming to produce an exhaustive list of all the murders which stained the Ptolemaic line. Assassination was de rigeur. The dynasty began well – Ptolemy I Soter died in his bed at the age of 84 – but no other Ptolemies were to be so fortunate. Cleopatra's suicide, and the assassination of her son and co-ruler Caesarion, brought to its conclusion a line that had been both glorious and cruel.

A sphinx said to represent Ptolemy XII Neos Dionysus Auletes, father of Cleopatra VII.

Head of Arsinoë II, sister and second wife of Ptolemy II Philadelphus.
© The American Numismatic Society

On the reverse, a horn of plenty and the inscription *Arsinoe Philadelphou*.
© The American Numismatic Society

FAMILY TREE
OF THE PTOLEMIES

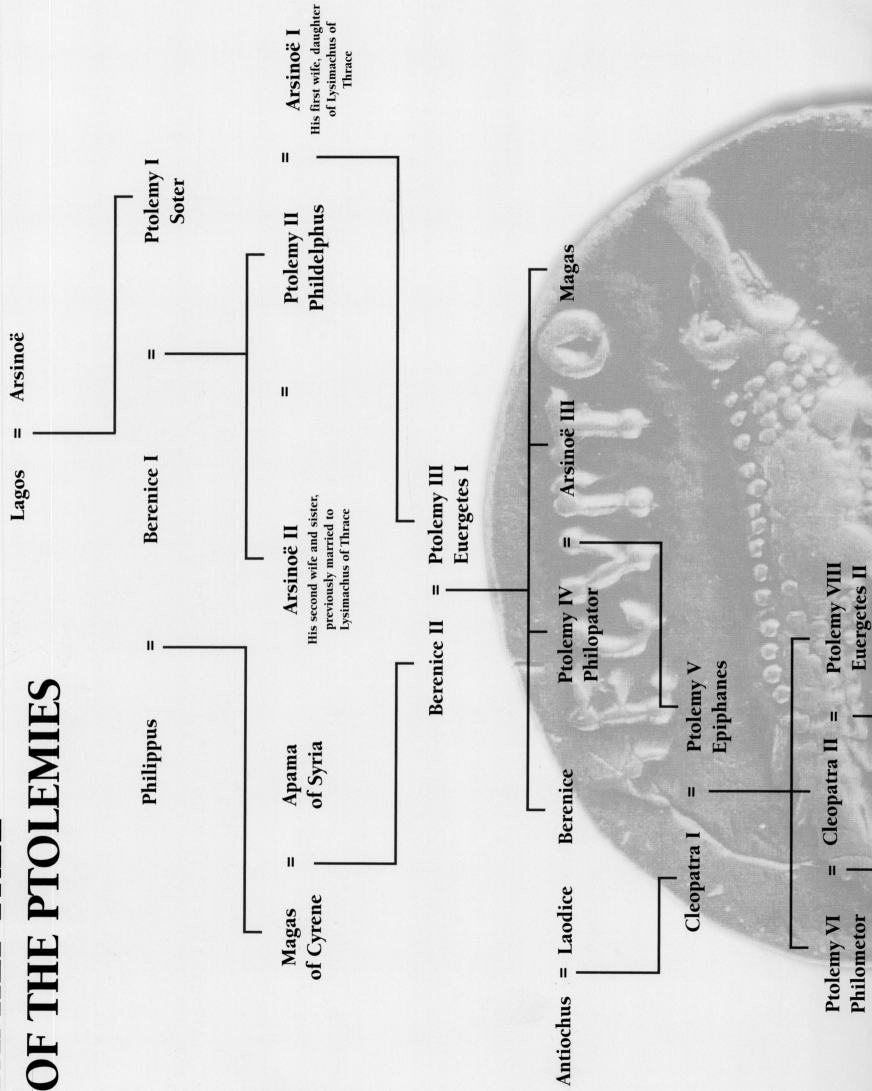

Lagos = Arsinoë

Ptolemy I
Soter

Berenice I = Arsinoë II
His second wife and sister,
previously married to
Lysimachus of Thrace

= Ptolemy II
Phildelphus

= Arsinoë I
His first wife, daughter
of Lysimachus of Thrace

Philippus =

Magas = Apama
of Cyrene   of Syria

Berenice II = Ptolemy III
Euergetes I

Magas

Arsinoë III = Ptolemy IV
Philopator

Antiochus = Laodice   Berenice

Cleopatra I = Ptolemy V
Epiphanes

Ptolemy VI   = Cleopatra II = Ptolemy VIII
Philometor   Euergetes II

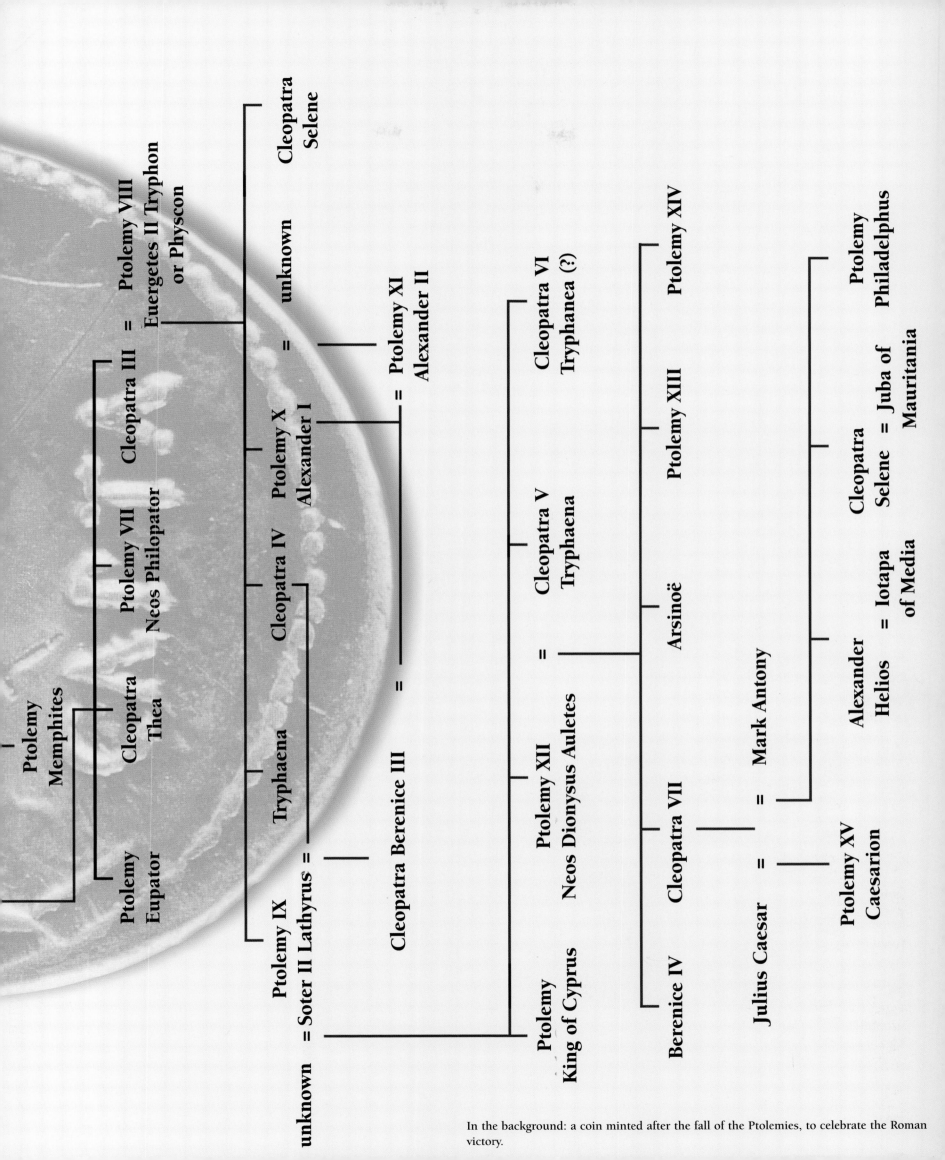

In the background: a coin minted after the fall of the Ptolemies, to celebrate the Roman victory.

The island of Antirhodos

Antirhodos is famous for the royal palace that stood there in the time of Cleopatra (69–30 BC),
but the island already played an important role in the Bay of Alexandria before Cleopatra's arrival. It is
probable, in fact, that there were already buildings on the island prior to the foundation of Alexandria, and
towards the middle of the 3rd century BC it was the site of major building projects.

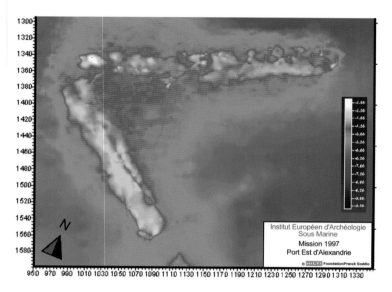

Island of Antirhodos: bathymetric map.

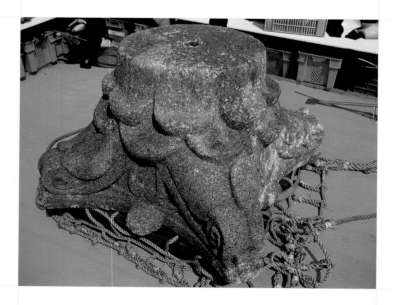

Sculpted architectural elements like this column base are
brought up on deck so that precise measurements can be taken.

T he island, which is made up of three branches, measures 350m at its longest point and 70m at its widest. The historian Strabo, who visited Alexandria four years after the death of Cleopatra, in 26 BC, describes Antirhodos – so named, he says, *as if it were the rival of Rhodes* – as an island situated *in front of the man-made harbour, possessing a royal palace and a small port.*

Cleopatra's palace

A great deal has been written about Cleopatra's palace and yet, properly speaking, Cleopatra had several palaces and the one she inhabited on the island of Antirhodos dated from well before her time. Cleopatra is particularly remembered for the ostentatious manner in which she decorated these royal residences. The description offered by the poet Lucan (39–65 AD) in his *Pharsalia* leaves the reader dazed: *Cleopatra surrounded herself with a flamboyant display of luxury on a scale previously unknown in Roman society. The place resembled a temple such as one would be unlikely to see even in more corrupt times. The panelled vaults were crammed with precious materials. Thick panels of gold concealed the woodwork. The palace shone with marble, and not just thin sheets of marble. There were solid blocks of agate and porphyry and throughout the palace there was an abundance of onyx underfoot. The vast door jambs were not simply overlaid with ebony from the shores of Lake Mareotis: the ebony stood in place of vulgar oak, serving as a support rather than an ornament to the dwelling. The galleries of the atrium were faced in ivory, and applied to the doors were the shells of Indian tortoises, hand painted and decorated with spots in each of which was set an emerald.*

Not a single tortoise shell set with emeralds is to be found on the sea-bed today – unsurprisingly. Remains of the palace itself, however, have been discovered, but the foundations, which are easy to date, were built in approximately 250 BC, well before Cleopatra's time. The palace had probably undergone numerous alterations and even been completely rebuilt since that time. It was situated at the centre of the island's widest branch, facing the town, on a huge paved esplanade of 6,000m^2. Inevitably it is at this point that the architectural remains are most numerous: column shafts made of red granite of various thicknesses (between 75 and 110cm) and sometimes decorated with a moulding; blocks of red granite, two of which (re-cut in order to be used again) carry hieroglyphic inscriptions; blocks of limestone, quarzite and basalt of various sizes. All these structures appear to

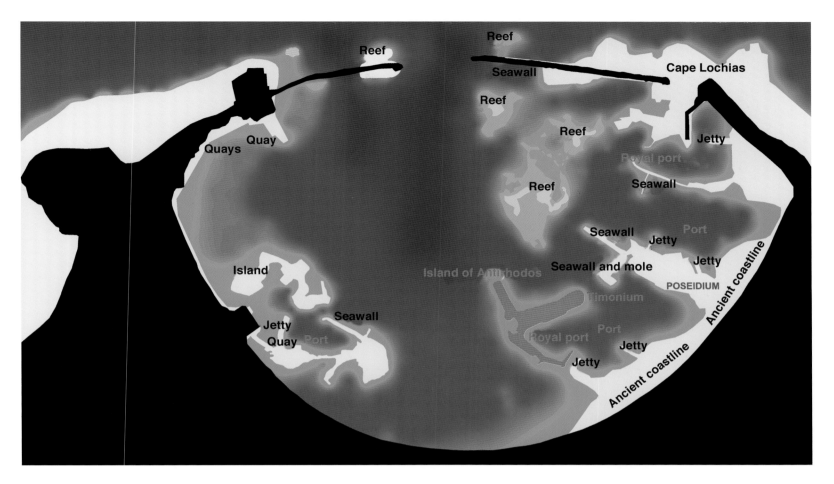

Map of the Portus Magnus, with the island of Antirhodos shown in red.

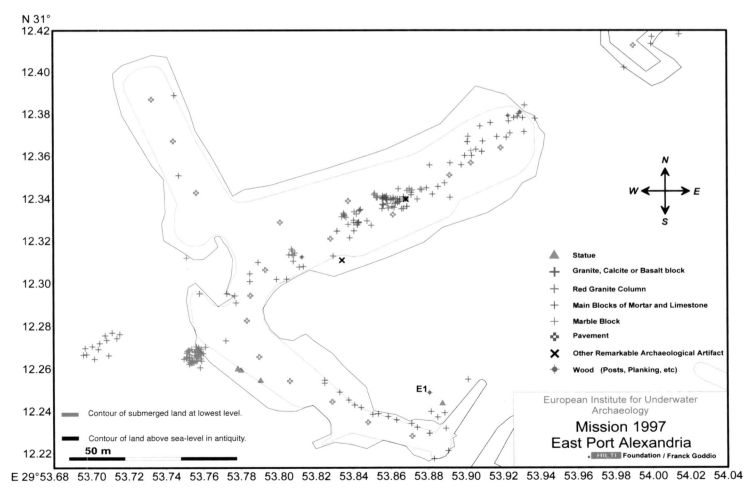

The island of Antirhodos with its central platform and the alignment of the axial colonnade.

Greek inscription revealed after cleaning the base of a statue discovered on the island of Antirhodos. These letters were carved almost 2,000 years ago, in the time of the Emperor Caracalla, who left his mark on columns that dated back much earlier than his reign.

have collapsed under the impact of an earthquake or landslide, shattering the paving at the point of fall and remaining for centuries in this position.

The eight Greek inscriptions were particularly revealing – seven were engraved in panels on column shafts and one on a marble block. The letters are narrow, cramped and elongated, and characteristic of the beginning of the 3rd century: they were therefore added very late. One of them dates from the reign of Commodus (180–192 AD); the others from the reign of Caracalla (211–217 AD). The palace was probably no longer standing by Caracalla's time, but the tyrant found another use for the esplanade – as a site for displaying seven statues carved in his own likeness.

This inscription is the oldest of those discovered, dating back to the reign of Commodus (180–192). The first line has been entirely effaced by hammering; the third simply indicates the day and the month.

M[arcus] Aurelius Commodus Antoninus Augustus, under Quintus Tineius Demetrius, prefect of Egypt, the 6 Tubi [1-2 January].

The inscription on the right can be dated precisely since it mentions the prefect of Egypt, Quintus Tineius Demetrius, who, from references in the papyri, we know to have filled that role between 189 and 190. It reveals for the first time the prefect's *praenomen*, which is written out in full instead of being abbreviated.

[In honour of the] master of earth and sea, sovereign of the universe, votary of Sarapis, eternally living, M[arcus] Aur[elius] Severus Antoninus, god Augustus.

This one-word fragment is the end of an inscription the remainder of which is missing. The style of the writing dates it to the beginning of the 3rd century AD.

…of Lykopolis…

Is this the Lycopolis in the delta, or the town of the same name on the borders of Middle and Upper Egypt, modern-day Asyut? The Greeks called the latter 'the wolf town' because the principal local divinity was Oupouaout, a black dog associated, like Anubis, with funerary rituals. Lycopolis/Asyut is also commonly regarded as the home of the famous Neo-Platonist philosopher Plotinus (born in 205 AD), who is reputed to have followed the teachings of Alexandria's rhetoricians as a young man.

The column shaft is broken at the top and all that remains of the inscription are two lines naming the dedicators and indicating the year, followed by the name of the emperor. The latter has been hammered, but the abbreviated *praenomen* is still legible as well as the initial A of the emperor's *nomen*.

The Romans and Alexandrians, year 20 of M[arcus] Aur[elius] Severus Antoninus [213 AD].

Caracalla, the monster who wanted to be Alexander

There is one point upon which all historians are in agreement: that the Emperor Caracalla was both ugly and mad, or at least prey to outbursts of violence bordering on madness. Alexandria was to feel the effects of one of his most unfortunate, and famous, fits of anger.

Son of the Emperor Septimius Severus, from the African city of Lepcis Magna, and of Julia Domna, daughter of the high priest of Emesa, in Syria, Caracalla was showered with honours from a very early age. At age 8 he adopted the name Marcus Aurelius and the title of Caesar. At 11, after accompanying his father on campaign during the second Parthian war, he received from the Senate the title of 'great conqueror of the Parthians'. At 20, during the expedition to Upper Brittany, Caracalla directed military operations, since his father had fallen seriously ill, and once more emerged as victor. When his father died Caracalla had been elected consul three times: he was only 23.

Head of Caracalla, discovered at Tanis. The emperor's squat forehead and air of fierce intransigence combine to create a thoroughly disagreeable impression (in no way alleviated by the absence of his nose). Graeco-Roman Museum, Alexandria.

Caracalla was a young man given to excess and all these exploits and honours inevitably went to his head, bolstering his dreams of greatness. His one objective in life was to achieve supreme power, even at the cost of eliminating all potential rivals, no matter how remote. His own brother Geta was one such rival and Caracalla had him assassinated in 212 AD, then massacred his followers – a mere 20,000 men. He also put to death anyone who mocked or made fun of him – those who accused him of committing incest with his mother (with whom he lived), for example, or those who joked about his appearance. One word spoken out of turn, and the speaker lost his head.

The emperor was short and ugly and hypersensitive. Driven by the urge to excel and conquer his natural limitations, Caracalla devoted himself to the most violent forms of physical exercise. According to the historian Dio Cassius, he was able single-handedly to slaughter 100 wild boars in a day. During military campaigns he deliberately endured great physical hardships, preferring to walk rather than ride, and carry his own arms, or even the army's emblems, which were laden with gold ornaments and due to their great weight usually reserved for the strongest of the foot soldiers. The troops applauded his courage and his simplicity, according to Herodian: *If a trench needed digging, or a bridge building, or a ditch filling, he was the first to start shovelling. He was the first to undertake anything that required manual effort or physical strength. His meals were frugal. Sometimes he even used wooden vessels for eating and drinking, and he would consume bread which he made himself as the need arose, crushing in his hands the requisite amount of wheat for one person and moulding it into a little cake, baking it in the embers of the fire, then eating it. He scorned all luxury and only availed himself of things that could be readily obtained by the simplest and poorest soldiers. And if they called him their companion rather than their emperor, he affected to be pleased by this.*

Caracalla was following the advice which Septimius Severus is said to have given his sons on his death bed: *Keep the peace, enrich your soldiers and do not trouble yourselves about the rest.* Caracalla in fact doubled his soldiers' wages, thereby placing a heavy burden on the public finances. Sharing power with his mother, he left the internal affairs to her and concentrated on the defence of his frontiers. Dio Cassius describes him as *philalexandrotatos* (a 'lover of Alexander') and his dream was to be a great commander on a par with his hero. Cassius claims that Caracalla even went so far as to write to the Senate that *the soul of Alexander had entered the body of Augustus [Caracalla] in order to assume a new and longer existence, since the first had been of short duration.*

Caracalla did not enjoy a long life, however, since he was assassinated at the age of 29, but it was a life filled with military expeditions, notably in Upper Germany in 213 AD, then, in 214 AD, across Asia Minor, where he presented himself as a *new Achilles* after visiting the tomb of the hero at Ilion. Caracalla arrived in Alexandria in the autumn of 215 AD, eager to visit the tomb of its founder and of his great idol, as well as the temple dedicated to Serapis, to whom he paid special homage. This visit was to end in disaster. The Alexandrians, known for their irreverence, apparently referred to Caracalla as *Achilles' and Alexander's little monkey* and called his mother Jocasta (the name of Oedipus' mother), holding them both up to ridicule. Such mockery was more than the emperor could bear. He was to avenge himself in a manner that was totally disproportionate to the supposed crime.

After his initial welcome at Alexandria, involving several days of uninterrupted festivities, he sent out an edict requiring all the young people of the city to assemble on the esplanade under the pretext of forming a Macedonian phalanx in honour of Alexander. Thousands of young people lined up confidently, surrounded by their families. The emperor walked up and down inspecting the ranks, bestowing praise here and there, while his army deployed around the crowd. Then, at a given signal, the soldiers suddenly bore down on the defenceless population, slaughtering every last person present and throwing their bodies into mass pits. Concluding his description of the episode, Herodian wrote: *The carnage was so great that the rivers of blood flowed across the esplanade and reddened the mouth of the Nile, though the latter was vast, reddening also the whole coast of Alexandria and its environs.* In order to suppress any opposition on the part of the remaining population and prevent groups of people from congregating, the emperor prohibited all public spectacles and banquets, built a wall cutting the city in two and erected surveillance towers. The army could thus be provisioned without any risk of public unrest, in readiness for the campaign that Caracalla was planning against the Parthians. The emperor was assassinated a year later, during this campaign.

He was to leave Alexandria seven statues in his likeness, erected on the island of Antirhodos, facing the city, and one deeply tragic memory.

Majestic sandstone statue of Caracalla conserved in Cairo Museum, representing the emperor as a pharaoh.

Section of a sunken palisade showing the remains of planks and a wooden pale. These ancient relics are vitally important, providing clear evidence that the site selected by Alexander was already occupied well before his arrival.

Wood that tells a story

We can only imagine what the royal palace was like, based on descriptions. Excavations on the island of Antirhodos, on the other hand, have enabled us to make concrete discoveries that tell us a great deal about the practical genius of those early architects. Thanks to the overall map, established in 1997, we can appreciate the situation in much the same way as they must have done. A series of reefs on the north-eastern side of the bay formed a natural breakwater, off which ships sailed after passing through the main fairway. They then had the choice of entering one of three ports, the largest of which, measuring 16 hectares, was closed to the west by the island of Antirhodos. If there was a strong wind blowing from the north-west, the island would have protected ships from the swell, its south-eastern coast forming a particularly sheltered little harbour. Remains of limestone embedded in mortar prove, moreover, that the coastline was originally organised as a series of quays. The whole of the northern end of the island, which is exposed to the open sea, is protected by large limestone blocks (averaging 110cm x 50cm x 50cm), some of which have been cut to size.

The most significant find, however, as regards the harbour facilities, is built not of granite or limestone, but of wood – a material exceptionally rare in Egypt, and yet one which has survived the centuries astonishingly well underwater. The eastern extremity of the island is made up of rock fills which slope gently towards the harbour channel. Beneath this rock, at a depth of 60cm, two rows of approximately parallel piles have been discovered, oriented along the axis of the island's main branch and spaced 1.5 to 1.8m apart. The southernmost row is constructed of piles with grooves, into which planks were slotted to form an underground pale. All these elements suggest that a quay once stood here.

A further piece of evidence relates to the piles of the southernmost row, which are set into a mortar base. Since the mortar could only dry in the open air, not underwater, we must conclude that this row was not therefore submerged at the time of construction, but must have constituted a small sheet-pile wall capable of supporting a fill of ungraded quarry materials; it was not until later that it sank beneath the water level.

The analysis of fragments of wood using radiocarbon dating provides another interesting insight. The piles, made of elm wood, appear to date from *circa* 410 BC, and the planks, which are made of pine, from 395 BC (allowing a margin of error of plus or minus 40 years) – in other words, prior to the construction of Alexandria.

The Saitic and Persian kings always subjected Greek commercial vessels to rigorous police and customs checks in the region of the future Alexandria, and a military post had been set up there. The Pharaohs were no less vigilant, but we know that they also made use of Greek mercenaries. It is possible that these mercenaries disembarked in the island's sheltered inner harbour and that the port facilities were therefore constructed (using that typical import, elm wood) for their benefit.

Formwork

Pieces of wood were also discovered during an examination of the area situated to the south-west of the central esplanade. These consisted of sections of beams measuring approximately 10cm x 12cm, as well as a huge formwork that was remarkably well preserved by the marine deposits. This formwork is constructed of horizontal planks held in place by transverse beams assembled with the help of dovetails and placed here and there flush with the natural rock in order to follow variations in ground level. Other beams, some vertical and some inclined, aided the block of mortar to retain its shape. The vertical faces of the formwork have disappeared, but they have left marks on the mortar itself.

The mortar, a mixture of slaked lime (limestone heated at 1,000 °C), sand and water, could only harden in the open air. So how could it be employed under water in the construction or surfacing of the quays? The builders' ingenious solution was to make a formwork, which they filled with sand up to water level. Mortar was poured on to the bed of sand, where it stood out of the water and could set in the open air. Once the mortar had set, the sides of the formwork were removed, releasing the sand and leaving the block of mortar in its final resting place. A similar technique involved a floating caisson (see diagram on p. 153). This procedure explains the presence of angled timbers held fast in the block, which were used to brace the caisson while it was being floated into position, and the remains of timber boxing underneath the block. The side-walls of the formwork would have been removed after the block was in place on the sea-bed.

A bed of river pebbles was spread on top of the surrounding natural limestone, and on top of this limestone paving was placed flush with the blocks of mortar: the builders were thus able to grade a large area of the island efficiently and economically while simultaneously constructing solid foundations capable of supporting considerable weight. According to radiocarbon analysis of the pine of the formwork, this ingenious construction dates back to *circa* 250 BC.

These wooden planks discovered beneath a block of mortar belong to formwork which was carbon dated to give an idea of the date of the quay's construction.

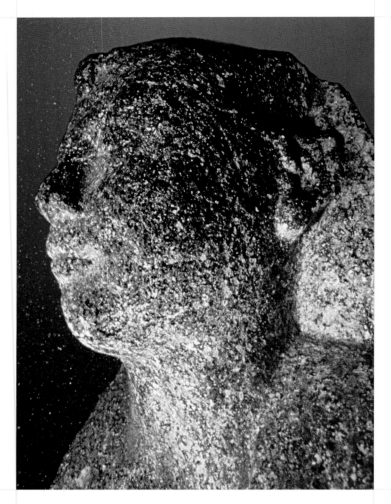

The entire surface of this sculpture has been eroded by long exposure to saltwater and grains of sand rubbing against it in the current, but the characteristics of the sphinx are still clearly visible.

Two sphinxes and a number of theories

The south-west slope of the island held some pleasant surprises for us: an impressive concentration of red granite column shafts, 95cm x 110cm in diameter and measuring 60m placed end to end, alongside a vast area of limestone paving and flagstones measuring 40cm x 40cm and 120cm x 55cm, respectively. This ancient esplanade had partially collapsed towards the sandy harbour bottom, and between the rubble and the paving still *in situ* we discovered two little gems: two sphinxes, which were astonishingly well preserved, one made of grey granite, slightly chipped on the right side (presumably at the time of its fall), and the other of diorite, missing only the extremities of its forepaws. The two sphinxes measure, respectively, 1.5m and 1.4m long.

Their elongated faces and soft features are intact, indicating that they were not deliberately overturned. Pieces of pottery discovered beneath the rubble date from between the 1st century BC and the 2nd century AD: the earthquake which caused the platform to collapse cannot therefore have occurred before this period.

In the Pharaonic tradition, sphinxes represent royal personages and the two statues are wearing the *nemes* or royal headdress with its two long flaps descending either side of the head on to the breastplate and the long cylindrical braid hanging down the creature's back. They are royal effigies mingling the Pharaonic tradition with Hellenistic principles relating to physiognomy and headdress. This mixed style is not attested before Ptolemy VI, so that we can safely say that the two sphinxes represent two late Ptolemies. The granite sphinx provides us with a further clue, since Ptolemy XII is traditionally represented, as here, with strands of hair escaping from beneath his *nemes*. Professor Zsolt Kiss has therefore identified this figure as the father of Cleopatra VII.

The other sphinx has not been identified. Why is its headdress different? Does it date from the same period as the first sphinx? Were they meant to appear together from the start – or were they only associated later? The two statues enable us to conclude, at any rate, that a temple – probably dedicated to Isis – once existed on the island of Antirhodos. A second find was to confirm this hypothesis.

A diver pays his respects to the diorite sphinx, so far unidentified, although it may represent one of the later Ptolemies.

*The granite sphinx
discovered on the western
coast of the island and
identified by its headdress
as Ptolemy XII, father of
Cleopatra VII.*

The statue of the priest of Isis carrying a Canopic vase, shortly after its discovery.

Our most beautiful discovery: the statue of the priest of Isis carrying a Canopic vase with Osiris' head emerging from it.

The priest carrying Osiris-Canopus

What was the most moving discovery for us at Alexandria? In answer to this question, we simply exchange smiles. No need for debate as the answer is unanimous: the priest.

Not far from the sphinxes lay a beautiful statue carved out of a dark granitoid, broken off at the level of the knees and measuring, in its present mutilated state, 1.5m. The figure is standing, dressed in a long pleated tunic with a cloak wrapped tightly around his upper body. His head is completely shaved and he is carrying a vase surmounted by a human head – two characteristics that enable us to identify him unequivocally as a priest of Isis, probably taking part in a procession, or at any rate a ritual ceremony of some description. The ancient texts specifically tell us that a priest carried the image of the sacred vase during processions in honour of the goddess Isis.

A priest was required, by his condition, to shave his head, moustache and beard in the interests of purity. The groove running across this man's brow should not therefore be interpreted as a bandeau, but rather as a deep furrow befitting the gravity of his office, for the face is that of a young man. The stopper of the vase is in the form of a man's head adorned with a beard and the royal *nemes*, with a fringe just visible beneath it – features which identify the vase as an Osiris-Canopus.

An ancient Greek legend recounts that a pilot of Menelaus, named Canopos, died from a snake bite and was buried at the mouth of the western branch of the Nile, leaving his name to a city that was then known in Egyptian as Pe-gouti. Pe-gouti/Canopus is the precise location where Isis is said to have discovered the 14th part of her husband and brother Osiris after his dismemberment by his brother Set. The story goes that Isis kept these pieces in a vase, and so the image of the vase is traditionally used to represent Osiris. Urns with anthropomorphic stoppers, representing the four sons of Horus, were also used to preserve embalmed viscera following mummification: one with a human head (Amset) for the liver, the second with a baboon's head (Api) for the lungs, the third with a dog's head (Douamoutef) for the stomach, and the fourth with a falcon's head (Kebehsenouf) for the intestines. Antiquaries in the 18th century erroneously extended the term to these funerary urns, and Egyptologists have retained the designation by convention. Here, however, there is no possible scope for confusion: what we are dealing with is a genuine Osiris-Canopus.

According to one theory, proper Osiris-Canopus vases were originally capable of holding floodwater from the Nile, which was associated with the fluids emanating from Osiris' body, but the preserved images of Osiris-Canopus, whether they are made of terracotta, limestone or bronze, were never intended to hold anything at all. They appear to have been used not as vessels, even for holy water, but as a representation of one of the divine aspects: 'Osiris in the jar'. This motif appears for the first time on Alexandrian coins during the second half of the 1st century and spread throughout the 2nd century, the last coins which bear it dating from the year 267 AD. It would be reasonable, however, to assume that a Canopic iconography existed prior to its attestation by the coinage, at the beginning of the imperial era, when a theology of the Canopus was developing around the theme of water as the source of life. Where Antirhodos is concerned, we can at least assume that a religious building existed on this site, as suggested by the presence of the two sphinxes.

The aesthetics of the statue display a mixture of Egyptian and Hellenistic influences: the priest's cloak falls from his shoulder in wide, flat folds familiar to us from representations of the Ptolemaic era, but the folds falling from below his forearms, rather than obeying conventional rules, correspond to the real tensions in the material as evoked by the wearer's movements, following an entirely Hellenistic style of representation.

The most interesting thing about the statue, however, is what it tells us regarding the potentially complex relationship between the priest and his god: a mixture, it appears, of love and fear, of tenderness and respect. Why, for instance, is the priest not holding the vase in his bare hands, but concealing his hands beneath his cloak instead? Is it from fear of contaminating the god or because such contact can be dangerous? His affection for Osiris, on the other hand, is unhesitating as he leans his cheek tenderly against the vase, his expression serene. It is worth remembering that, according to the legend, Osiris was first and foremost an enlightened sovereign who was known as Ounophris, 'the Good Being'.

The statue of the priest standing between the two sphinxes, after they were re-erected in situ. This magical scene required five days to photograph before the correct lighting effects could be achieved.

Detail: note the tender and reverential expression of the priest as he holds Osiris' head against his cheek.

Isis and Osiris

Isis is the most famous of the Egyptian divinities. Goddess of the dead, protector of life, wife, mother, sorceress, she gave rise to a Graeco-Roman cult, traces of which are to be found on the island of Antirhodos, where the ruins of a sanctuary to Isis have been discovered.

When Osiris succeeded his father Geb to the throne of Egypt, he married his sister Isis. They were the first divine couple to rule as sovereigns and live among mortal men. After 28 years of a happy and prosperous reign, Osiris was celebrating his victorious return from a long and successful military campaign when he became the victim of a plot organised by his brother Set. Set had a wooden chest which he said he would give to anyone who filled it when he lay down in it. Osiris duly lay down… and Set sealed up the chest and promptly had it thrown into the Nile. The distraught Isis cut her hair and rent her clothes and departed in search of her beloved husband.

The chest travelled to the shores of Phoenicia, where it was washed up at the foot of a tamarisk tree. The tree, as it grew, encompassed the chest in its trunk. When it was cut down to provide timber for the palace of the king of Byblos, a 'divine' odour emanated from it, betraying the presence of the chest within. Isis heard news of this strange occurrence and hastened to the spot, where she was able to confirm that the body was indeed that of Osiris. She took the chest back to Egypt, where she kept it hidden in the Bouto marshes, and succeeded in uniting herself with Osiris' remains and giving birth to their son, Horus. Set accidentally discovered the body while he was out hunting and viciously hacked it into 14 pieces, which he scattered about the countryside.

Undaunted, Isis took up the search again and succeeded in collecting together all the pieces of her dead husband and putting them in a vase. She found the last piece at the city of Canopus – hence the name Osiris-Canopus which was later given to those representations of a vase with the head of Osiris.

Anubis mummified the body of Osiris, and Isis, helped by Nephthys, Thoth and Horus, succeeded in breathing life into him with the use of magic formulas – the first instance of a dead person receiving the embalming rite destined to procure eternal life.

Fully restored to life and no longer fearing death, Osiris could have reclaimed the throne of Egypt, but instead he ceded it to his son Horus, preferring to dwell in the kingdom of the dead. Horus, the falcon-headed god with the body of a man, was to provide the model for all future kings.

From myth to cult

Osiris was originally a local god associated with the northern town of Busiris, but the cult of Osiris as god of the dead encompassed the whole of Egypt. Isis was the most popular divinity in the entire Egyptian pantheon, representing the wife whose love knows no limits, the quintessential mother (often depicted nursing her child and providing the inspiration for Egypt's first images of the Virgin Mary) and the sorceress with access to secret knowledge.

It was in this last role that she particularly fascinated the Greeks. From the end of the 4th century, and especially in the course of the 2nd century BC, small communities of Greeks and in some cases entire cities developed their own individual cult of Isis. Alexandria adopted her as patron of its dynasty and sailors. A kind of Isis religion grew up within the Greek community, based on the Osirian myths, but adapting them to Greek tastes. What were at the outset magic rituals designed to ensure eternal life according to the divine model were transformed by the Greeks into a universal doctrine of salvation. Sanctuaries were built, re-using Egyptian architectural elements, but the statues of the gods followed the Greek aesthetic and rituals were conducted in the Greek language. It was thanks to this that the cult of Isis spread through Europe, beginning with Rome and the Emperor Caligula: the large temple to Isis built by Caligula on the Campus Martius in the course of his reign (37–41 AD) was to stand until the end of the pagan era.

According to the legend, Isis assembled the scattered pieces of her husband's body and placed them in a vase at Canopus, where she discovered the 14th and last piece. Osiris, in the guise of Osiris-Canopus, subsequently came to be represented by a vase with an anthropomorphic stopper like the one the priest at Alexandria is holding.

Statue of a Ptolemaic king in the guise of a white marble Hermes, discovered on the island of Antirhodos.

A white marble Hermes

On the southern branch of the island, at the base of a mass of fallen earth, we were met by a god – or his headless effigy at least. This large white marble body measured 1.7m in its current mutilated state. Not only the head, but also the arms were missing, and the legs were broken just below the left calf and in the middle of the right thigh. The original statue must have measured around 2m, being only slightly taller than life-size. A hole where the left arm would have been attached suggests that the statue had been repaired. A metal tenon, located inside the cavity, must have supported a piece of white marble added at a later date to represent the forearm after the original arm was broken – proof of the statue's great age.

The figure is naked except for a cloak (*himation*) pinned across its right shoulder – a detail that identifies the figure with Hermes. This iconographic arrangement in the tradition of Polyclitus is attributed to the late Hellenic period, although some experts regard the *himation* as a Roman characteristic.

Hermes is commonly represented in Ancient Egypt. In his role as messenger of Olympus and legendary inventor of alchemy, he is associated with the god Thoth, who fulfils the same functions. Over and above its divine associations, however, the statue may also have implications in terms of royal propaganda. The Ptolemies were associated with certain gods, and among these Hermes was a particular favourite, as demonstrated by the numerous bronze figurines representing him as a warrior, wearing the royal *nemes* on his head. No marble statues have been found, however, representing a Ptolemy in the form of Hermes, although such statues were popular with the Roman emperors from Augustus onwards.

So how are we to date this sculpture? The erosion caused by its lengthy sojourn on the harbour bottom makes any analysis difficult, but the softly sculpted effect of the chest is typical of Hellenistic rather than Roman workmanship, which tends towards rigid lines and sharper relief. If the statue's head had not disappeared, and if it had been decorated with lotus petals, as in the case of the bronze figurines, it would have been tempting to identify this Hermes with Ptolemy III; but the absence of the head makes it impossible for us to say.

This beautiful gold ring rewarded the efforts of divers clearing sediment in the vicinity of a wreck found off the island of Antirhodos.

One last trail: the wreck

We had found a palace, a sanctuary, and a number of quays, and thanks to these architectural fragments a picture of the island was beginning to emerge as it may once have been a few centuries previously… and even a little longer ago. Most importantly, however, the island also sheltered a harbour – a harbour which was particularly well protected, as we have seen, by its southern and eastern branches. It was in the middle of this little harbour that we discovered a wreck: a large ship whose wooden remains (well preserved by the silt) have been the subject of careful study. According to carbon dating and the analysis of material discovered in the vicinity, pottery and jewellery in particular, the ship probably dates from the end of the 1st century BC or the 1st century AD. The wreck is destined to be the subject of a separate publication; but what we can say here is that searches in the area uncovered two magnificent gold rings…

A second ring was discovered at the site of the wreck in Antirhodos' royal harbour, lying between two ribs.

Cleopatra

Few women in the course of history have exercised such a profound impact as Cleopatra (69–30 BC), queen of Egypt and mistress, successively, of Julius Caesar and of Mark Antony, who dreamed of making Alexandria the rival of Rome. Her enduring image is of a seductress, certainly, but also a clever strategist who succeeded in restoring the fortunes of Egypt without shedding any blood but her own.

Was Cleopatra beautiful? Dio Cassius (155–235 AD), an important official in the senatorial hierarchy, who settled in Italy in order to gather material for his *History of Rome*, tells us (42, 34, 4 *sqq.*) that Cleopatra was the most beautiful woman who ever lived. Plutarch (c. 46–120 AD), in his *Life of Caesar* (49, 1–5), speaks not of her beauty but of her grace (*charis*), which indicates that she was charming, but does not imply that she was beautiful; instead he praises in particular her intellectual qualities. In his *Life of Antony* (27, 35) he writes: *It is said that her beauty in itself was not incomparable or of a kind to instil wonder in those who beheld her, but in private intercourse with others she exercised an irresistible attraction, and her general appearance, coupled with her pleasing conversation and the natural grace which imbued her every word, had the effect of piercing her interlocutor like a thorn. When she spoke, the very sound of her voice gave pleasure. Her*

Vol. V.   ALEXANDRIE.

VUE DE L'OBÉLISQUE APPELLÉ AIGUILLE DE CLÉOPATRE ET DE LA TOUR DITE DES ROMAINS, PRISE DU SUD-OUEST.

View of the obelisk known as Cleopatra's Needle, taken from the *Description de l'Égypte*, vol. V, plate 32. © Photo RMN, Gérard Blot

tongue was like a many-stringed instrument, on which she played with ease in the language of her choice, since there were very few Barbarians with whom she required an interpreter: she responded without help to the majority among them, to the Ethiopians, for example, and the Troglodytes, the Hebrews, Arabs, Syrians, Medes and Parthians. It is said that she also knew several other languages, whereas the kings, her predecessors, had not even taken the trouble to learn Egyptian and some of them had even forgotten Macedonian.

One thing is certain: that she knew how to please, succeeding in seducing the seasoned dictator Julius Caesar when she was only 21 and he was 54. The manner of her arrival at Caesar's palace was a stroke of genius. Abandoning her exile in response to the general's summons, Cleopatra turned up with a single friend, the Sicilian Apollodorus, and concealed herself in a bundle of bed linen, in which she stretched out full length – a detail that confirms one other thing we know about Cleopatra: that she was both small and slight. She then leapt off her bearer's shoulders, giving Caesar to believe that she was a young boy – a fact that would not have displeased him, in the light of his sexual inclinations. We may reasonably suppose that Caesar recognised the young woman's courage and warmth, and that the two of them did not spend the entire night talking politics (Plutarch, *Life of Caesar*, 49, 1–3). Politics soon reasserted its rights, however, and Caesar restored Cleopatra to her former position as co-regent, reconciling her with her younger brother.

Queen of Egypt without a single drop of Egyptian blood

Cleopatra's father, Ptolemy XII Neos Dionysus Auletes, was a Greek like the rest of the Ptolemies. On his death in 51 BC, he had bequeathed the kingdom of Egypt to his oldest son, Ptolemy XIII, then aged 10, and to his daughter Cleopatra VII, aged 17, with the intention that the two should marry. Pompey, however, had appropriated Auletes' will to prevent any opposition from the Senate to his wishes. The situation in Egypt was critical – there were food shortages, tensions were rife between high officials in the administration, and schemes were afoot to set the young Ptolemy XIII against his wife and sister. Cleopatra was forced to flee to Syria to rally support. Then Pompey, defeated by Caesar at Pharsalus, sought refuge in Egypt, where he was murdered, and Cleopatra was able to take advantage of his death. Caesar, who disembarked at Alexandria three days after the death of his rival, wept when he was brought

Pompey's head and buried it in the grove of Nemesis that skirts the eastern wall of the city.

Cleopatra's dream: to reign over a new Athens

After Caesar, Mark Antony became Cleopatra's lover. Cleopatra's dream was to restore the kingdom of the Ptolemies and to prevent it becoming annexed to Rome. Indeed, she envisaged herself reigning over the entire Roman Empire from Alexandria, and Alexandria itself as the new Athens of the south.

It was to this extravagant ambition no doubt that she owed her downfall. When, in the autumn of 37 AD, Antony set sail for Corfu in pursuit of this Oriental dream, he took the decision to break with Rome, eager, like Caesar 10 years earlier, to restore the empire of the Ptolemies rather than to see Egypt become a province of Rome. Where Rome was concerned, Egypt possessed a particularly powerful weapon: it served Rome as a granary and could therefore starve Rome if it chose. Be that as it may, Antony was defeated by the Parthians and forced to make a miserable retreat, returning to Alexandria with Cleopatra's ships, so dashing all hopes of

Coin with the head of Cleopatra VII as Aphrodite, holding her son Ptolemy XV Caesarion.
© The American Numismatic Society

Caesar Returns Cleopatra to the Throne of Egypt, Pietro Berrettini, 1596–1669. Reproduced with the permission of the Réunion des Musées Nationaux.
© Photo RMN, Lagiewski

The Death of Cleopatra,
Alessandro Turchi, 1578–1649.
Reproduced with the permission
of the Réunion des Musées
Nationaux.
© Photo RMN, C. Jean

turning the Orient into a Ptolemaic empire run on federal lines, with its centre at Alexandria.

In 31 AD, Antony's defeat at the battle of Actium, at the entrance to the gulf of Ambracia (today Arta, in Greece), by the naval forces of Agrippa and Octavian, the future Augustus, was the final nail in the coffin. Rather than yield to Augustus – who, despite her entreaties, was determined to regard Cleopatra as part of the spoils of war – the queen committed suicide by stinging herself with an asp concealed in a basket of figs. She was 39 years old. Antony was already dead, having committed suicide at the age of 53. And so the extraordinary life of the great Cleopatra was terminated by a premature and violent death.

Bust of Cleopatra, Giorgio-
Giulio Clovio, 1498–1578.
Reproduced with the
permission of the Réunion
des Musées Nationaux.
© Photo RMN, Michèle Bellot

Divers admiring the statue of the priest guarded by the two sphinxes after they were replaced in situ.

The ancient coastline of the Portus Magnus

The 'ancient coastline' is the term used to describe the submerged coastline, as far as it has been possible to trace it, from Cape Lochias, halfway along the corniche, from the east to the south of the Portus Magnus. The submerged floor of the ancient shoreline is covered with an almost continuous series of stone blocks juxtaposed in a haphazard fashion – evidence that this was once a densely built area. Our attention was particularly attracted by a number of statues, which enabled us to take our first small step towards reconstructing the royal quarters.

I t is difficult to trace, with any certainty, the outline of the ancient coastline such as it must have appeared in Ptolemaic times. Three factors are responsible for modifying it: the instances of subsidence that have occurred since the 4th and 5th centuries, the rise of the sea level and the work undertaken at the end of the 19th century and the beginning of the 20th to raise the level of the shoreline. The obelisk erected in 13 BC and known as 'Cleopatra's Needle' is proof of these changes: in 1879, the year of its removal to New York, the monument was photographed in front of a building which is still standing today, approximately 120m from the present shoreline (see p. 21). In the photograph, however, the obelisk stands right next to the shore, as it does in a drawing by Dejuine dating from between 1798 and 1801. When the coast road was built, following the monument's removal, the construction work must therefore have encroached on more than 100m of sea. Happily for us, the submerged area was not entirely engulfed, since the ancient coastline can still be observed beneath the water almost as far as the southernmost point of the corniche, where it disappears beneath the modern embankments.

On this drawing executed by Dejuine at the end of the 18th century, Cleopatra's Needle is situated near the shoreline, whereas the building seen to its right is currently 120m from the sea, evidence that the configuration of the coastline has altered in the intervening centuries.

Along the whole eastern stretch of the Portus Magnus, the ancient coastline (shown here in red) is visible a few metres beneath the water.

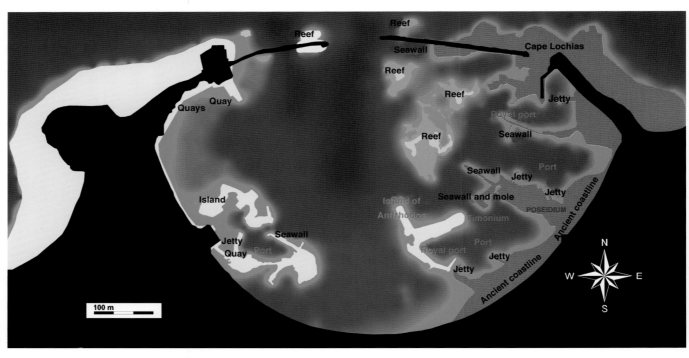

The remains of quays and esplanades are visible at various points, particularly on a level with the island of Antirhodos, where a substantial mole (130m x 30m) juts into the sea, paved with limestone (some of the individal stones measuring as much as 100cm x 50cm). This mole bends sharply to the north-east opposite the island's jetty. Up and down the whole coast numerous remains have been found, several hundred artefacts having been cleaned of their limestone deposits and examined to date.

The density of archaeological finds in the area testifies to the large number of buildings that stood along this eastern shoreline, as Strabo tells us: *All these buildings form a continuous construction, together with the port and even those buildings which extend beyond the port*. They comprise the *basileia* (royal buildings) quarter, which in Roman times was known as the *brucheion*. North of the great mole, however, the remains display no apparent architectural coherence and we may suppose that there were no buildings located here, but that this was the site of a quarry.

Numerous red granite capitals, column bases and shafts have been discovered along the entire length of the coastline; also limestone, basalt and quartzite blocks, beams engraved with panels of hieroglyphics, and sections of paving. A number of statues have also been discovered.

It is these statues which are particularly intriguing. The shattered columns may encourage a state of reverie and delineate, in our imagination, a space that was once inhabited; but to come face to face, on the sea-bed, with an ibis, a snake, a falcon head or the head of a pharaoh, makes us dramatically aware that human beings really did live here and left in the stone the traces of a religious and artistic sensibility that is quite simply... human. Even after months of diving, in all weathers, with varying success, such encounters are always emotionally charged.

Block of granite inscribed with hieroglyphs, seen here after an initial clean.

Diver swimming over a field of columns, part of the ancient coastline.

Outlines of the past

When Alexander landed where he did on the coast of Egypt and resolved to build the future city of Alexandria, he was taking an extraordinarily bold step: the topography of the area was unfavourable to such a plan, and the soil so arid that it was difficult to imagine how it could provide the resources to fulfil the needs of an entire city. And yet the conqueror's city was to be unrivalled in terms of both size and splendour.

To understand the reasons which led to the construction of Alexandria on the site chosen by Alexander the Great, we need to examine whether the ancient coastline offered any other possibilities.

There is a science known as historical geography which enables us to trace the ancient configuration of a country starting from current observation. This retrospective physical geography, as Roger Dion has described it, involves placing a town in its geographical context and working back from the present picture in an attempt to establish the ancient contours of the region. When we are dealing with a harbour, however, as in the case of Alexandria, the configuration of the ancient coastline poses a fundamental problem.

Since the time of the Roman Empire, several sections of the shoreline and the more prominent outlets of branches of the Nile have been submerged as a result of subsidence. Despite this, however, the topographical configuration and physical ecology of Egypt's Mediterranean coast were not radically different in Alexander's time from the way they appeared centuries later, prior to the transformations wrought by the creation of the high dam. We need only glance at an 18th-century map of the area to grasp how inauspicious the coastline of the delta was to sailors and why it was regarded as particularly dangerous by the Greeks. The Greek historian Diodorus Siculus, a contemporary of Ptolemy XII, summed up the situation as follows. Firstly, there was the distance: even supposing one took the most direct route, anyone coming from the Aegean or the Pelopponnese had to reckon with an extremely long crossing. Secondly, Egypt's shores offered no suitable anchorages. Between Paraetonium (Marsa Matruh) and Joppa (Jaffa in Palestine), the only safe haven was to be found at Pharos. The coastline, moreover, was very low and almost entirely bereft of natural seamarks, swept by cross currents and bordered by sandbanks, both of which increased the risks of shipwreck or of running aground. Anyone who did somehow succeed in landing on this deserted and uninhabitable strip of coastline found, as they pushed further inland, lakes and ponds choked with reed brakes and forests of papyrus, where a primitive and warlike folk sustained a living by gathering fruits and raising cattle. It would have been impossible to establish a permanent trading post, or *emporium*, here as happened elsewhere on barbarian shores. And the Egyptians themselves did nothing to render this quasi no-man's-land in any way less inhospitable to strangers.

These coasts, being virtually impassable, were deeply inconvenient for Greek, Carian and Phoenician traders and corsairs, while for the Egyptians they represented an effective system of defence, the only ways in and out of which were provided by the main branches of the Nile. Moreover, during the Pharaonic era (and later), the governors of Egypt exercised strict control over these distant fringes and over the mouths of the Nile, although they set up their control posts and their own harbour installations up-river from the lakes and marshes (whose unruly inhabitants served periodically as auxiliaries in the Pharaoh's army). During the 2nd millennium BC, most of Egypt's commercial relations with the Aegean world were conducted via Cyprus and the coast of the Levant. From the 8th century BC, the situation changed. The Greeks were by now expanding their horizons to the full and sailing the high seas, using the winds from the north to sweep them towards the coasts of Libya and the westward coasts of Lower Egypt, then skirting round to reach the Canopic mouth of the Nile, where they were subjected to controls and taxes at Thonis by the king's administration. The sheltered anchorage at Pharos provided an opportune stopping point before making their entry into Egypt.

It is worth bearing in mind that the advantages and disadvantages of the site chosen for the future city were long known to Greek mariners and travellers, well before Alexander's arrival. They were known to soldiers who came as military colonists in the service of the Saitic kings, to merchants who came to trade at Naucratis, to crews in the Athenian confederation allied with the Egyptians against the Persians, and to mercenaries recruited by the last indigenous Pharaohs.

When a dam was constructed at the head of the delta in order to control the floodwaters of the Nile it completely altered the hydrographic map of the western province, which subsequently received its water from the Raya de Behera, a canal dug in 1860, the source of which lay to the north of the village of Khatatbeh. If we wish to re-draw the hydrographic map as it would have appeared in antiquity, we need to disregard the modern drains. The layout of these drains is rectilinear and the best indicator of the age of a watercourse is the extent to which it meanders. The construction of the dam affected the cultivation of crops (depending as this does on irrigation), and the Alexandrian countryside is profoundly different now from how it appeared in antiquity. There are fields of rice and cotton and plantations of trees, and the mounds (*kiman*) previously marking the site of human settlements have been destroyed, many of them dug open and emptied of precious *sebbakh* (manure derived from various types of detritus), so that where there were once hills there are now only holes in the ground. Some of the *kiman* contained limestones and where these were uncovered lime kilns soon disposed of the remaining vestiges. With the arrival of the bulldozers and the construction of new roads the final changes were wrought and Alexandria was transformed into the modern city of today.

As we have noted, Alexandria was not considered to be in Egypt, but 'near Egypt' or, if one prefers, 'on the edge of Egypt'.

The narrow band of limestone, all rock and sand, bathed by the salty waters of the Mediterranean, was scarcely favourable to the growth of vegetation. In the 17th and 18th centuries, at a time when the approaches to Alexandria and its watercourses were suffering from several centuries of neglect, travellers commented on the painful sterility of the landscape, while also noting the existence of beautiful palm plantations on the Aboukir peninsula. In the 19th century the reconstruction of a canal channelling the waters of the Nile into Alexandria graced the city and its western suburbs with splendid gardens. In point of fact, during antiquity, the same arid strip of land was bathed by the waters of Lake Mareotis to the south, and these were annually renewed by the flooding of the Nile, while under the Ptolemies there were parks, groves and funeral gardens throughout the city thanks to the construction of a canal and a system for pumping the water.

Every Greek city comprised a *polis*, that is the city properly speaking, and a *chora*, or territory on which it depended for the production of its foodstuffs. Alexander and his successors succeeded in turning Egypt itself into Alexandria's *chora*, all the city's requirements arriving there either by road or by canal. The grid layout of the city, dear to Hippodamos of Miletus, was not an innovation, since it already existed at Piraeus in Attica, at Olynthus in Chalcidicum, at Priene in Asia Minor and at Magnesia on the River Maeander. It was at Alexandria, however, that the simplicity of the Hellenic legacy received its most original treatment.

Alexander the Great in his chariot, drawn by four elephants. Reverse side of a gold coin from the time of Ptolemy I Soter.

115

Agathodaimon

A mysterious object awaited us at the northern end of the peninsula: a coiled serpent, 30cm long, with its head missing – the only sculpture of its type to have been found in Pharaonic statuary to date. It is not the choice of creature which is surprising; rather the manner in which it is depicted. In two-dimensional representations the snake is either lying flat on the ground, crawling, raising its head, undulating, or forming a figure of eight. A serpent god known as Agathodaimon ('the good spirit') was worshipped in the Graeco-Roman religion of Egypt and corresponds to the Egyptian god Shai, 'destiny'. Every home and every town had its guardian spirit, responsible for the happiness and wellbeing of the inhabitants. Agathodaimon was the guardian of Alexandria, guarantor of the prosperity of the city and its inhabitants, and a famous temple was dedicated to him there in the Graeco-Roman era.

Images of the serpent god are extremely common in the Hellenistic-style iconographic repertory of the period, where he is featured on bas-reliefs, encircling a vase or an altar. The Agathodaimon found on Alexandria's ancient coastline has a cavity at the top which does not extend the full depth of the sculpture and is too small to have served as a receptacle for offerings. It may originally have enshrined some other object. On 2nd- and 3rd-century coins Agathodaimon is sometimes shown encircling poppies, a club (an attribute of Heracles) or a *caduceus* (the rod of Hermes, a staff entwined with two serpents). Whatever the cavity was for, there is every likelihood that the sculpture marks the site of a temple, and that it was the guardian of that temple.

This coiled serpent with its head missing is an Agathodaimon or 'good spirit', guardian of Alexandria.

The headless ibis

Another sacred animal was discovered in the same area as the serpent: a fairly large statue of an ibis, 45cm long and 28cm high. Although the head has disappeared, the creature is immediately recognisable as an ibis from the shape of its body and in particular its long, slim feet and widely spaced digits terminating in short claws. The ibis is sacred to Thoth and as such was widely represented in Egypt, enduring into the Graeco-Roman period, when Thoth was associated with Hermes. Thoth is the god of knowledge, wisdom and time (as a countdown to death), the scribe of the gods and simultaneously the god of scribes, or writing, responsible for setting down the results of the weighing of souls after death. Representing him three-dimensionally was problematic, however: how was one to sculpt in stone such a thin neck, such a pointed bill and such long feet? Where the feet were concerned, the trick was to represent the bird resting, as here, planted on a base: the feet are tucked up under the body, delicately carved but attached nevertheless to the rectangular support. The bird of Thoth is similarly represented in numerous votive bronzes dedicated by private individuals during the Saitic or Persian epochs and in wooden figurines attached to boxes serving as coffins for mummified ibis. As for the head and neck of the bird, these were most frequently constructed from bronze and attached to a body carved out of stone or wood, as in the case of the ibis from Hermopolis conserved in the Louvre. It is probable that the Alexandrian statue was constructed in the same fashion, the head and neck forming a single piece that was added later. In terms of its dimensions and the treatment of the body, lacking any details as regards plumage, the resemblance between the Paris ibis and the Alexandrian find is striking.

A work of average quality, carved in vulgar limestone, this image of the wise god Thoth-Hermes was no doubt made by a local artist of the Hellenistic period, though it takes its inspiration from strictly Egyptian imagery. We can assume that it stood inside a religious building, not far from the shore of the eastern harbour. Both its size and its shape preclude the possibility that it figured as part of the construction materials: along with the other statues it probably marked the site of sanctuaries that were later looted.

The headless ibis, sacred bird of the god Thoth-Hermes, discovered during excavations of the ancient coastline.

The famous wood and metal ibis (right) conserved in the Louvre (E. 17375) is remarkably similar to the Alexandrian find: in both cases, the bird is shown with its head raised and its feet tucked under its body and resting on a base. We can reasonably assume that the Alexandrian ibis' head and neck were also made of metal.

Divers uncovering a colossal head made of grey granite.

The head of a royal colossus

Several artefacts have been discovered on the coast facing the island of Antirhodos, notably a badly damaged basalt sphinx measuring 1.9m in length. The creature's face and its forefeet are missing, but we can guess that its head was crowned with the royal *nemes*, although we are unable to identify which sovereign it represents. One of the most interesting finds in this area, however, is a large sculpture carved out of grey granite, which was discovered lying on its side, partially buried. The visible part of the sculpture was covered with white deposits which we had to scrape off, but once these were removed, a wonderful surprise lay in store for us – a giant head, 80cm high, which must have formed part of a statue measuring some 5m. All that remains of the original statue is the head wearing the royal *nemes*, the neck and the upper part of the shoulders. The nose is broken and the lips have been flattened. Above each ear a cylindrical hole may have served to pin a metal, perhaps gold, band in place so that it encircled the forehead like a diadem. Although a slight convexity in the centre of the forehead suggests a broken frontal ornament, there is no sign of the *uraeus*, the sacred serpent represented on the headdress of ancient Egyptian kings and gods. Despite the absence of this royal attribute, the substantial size of the figure proves that it is in fact a royal effigy. And what better place to erect such a colossus than on the sea front, dominating the royal harbours?

Who could this have been? The headdress provides a valuable clue. The presence of strands of hair creeping out from beneath the *nemes* suggests that we may be dealing here with Ptolemy V or Ptolemy VI or one of their successors, but the regular and somewhat schematic fringe is a far cry from the flowing and disorderly strands represented in portraits of these two sovereigns. This combination – while remaining consistent with the Pharaonic tradition – is reminiscent rather of the manner in which the Roman emperors chose to be represented. The Emperor Augustus (63 BC–14 AD) was first identified, who, it should be remembered, set himself up not as the conqueror of the Ptolemies, but rather as the continuator of their administration, religion, ideology and art. The absence of the *uraeus* could be interpreted as a sign of moderation in the adoption of Pharaonic insignia imbued with divine associations. Today, however, it is generally agreed that the colossus can be identified as Caesarion, son of Julius Caesar and Cleopatra, the perfect example of a union between the Egyptian and Roman worlds, as borne out by the aesthetics of the piece.

To begin with, the colossus was just a huge formless block: there was no sign of a face until the limestone deposits had been removed.

The size of this head tells us at once that it belongs to a royal personage, while the strands of hair passing, Greek fashion, beneath the Pharaonic nemes almost certainly identify him as a Ptolemy. After close scrutiny, the colossus was finally identified as Ptolemy XV, better known by the name of Caesarion, the son of Cleopatra and Julius Caesar.

119

Diver treading the same ground that the Alexandrians trod in the time of Cleopatra, following in the footsteps of the great queen 2,000 years on.

An area littered with broken columns like this is described as a 'field of columns'. They are scattered as if a giant hand has knocked them over. Could it have been an earthquake or tidal wave? Gradually we come to understand the devastation suffered by the ancient city.

A Pharaoh's foot and a falcon-headed sphinx

The other exceptionally large sculpture concealed along this section of the coast is a 70cm high falcon head which must have belonged to a statue of similar dimensions to those of the colossus. The squat head is broken off at the level of the neck. The eye, which is very prominent, is surmounted by a long fold of stone forming the superciliary arch, attached above which and curving outwards is the wig of the bird. Visible on the creature's temple is a large human ear, which overlaps the wig. The latter, formed of large strands that frame the head, characterises all the divinities in traditional Egyptian iconography, whether these are represented in the form of humans or animals. The statue therefore represents a divine being whose nature is expressed by the falcon, which leaves us with several possibilities: Re-Horakhti, one of the three forms of the sun; Horus, son of Isis and Osiris, prototype of the Pharaoh worshipped under different names in different cities; Montu the warrior or, possibly, Sopdu the master of Asia. There is no way of knowing which of these is correct. The only hypothesis which can clearly be rejected is that the head formed part of a statue representing the falcon in its entirety, since if this had been the case, the statue would not have been wearing a wig. According to Professor Yoyotte, the figure may be a large hieracosphinx (hawk-headed sphinx) or a crocodile sphinx, and is unlikely to predate the 7th or 6th century BC. It is impossible to know whether the sculpture was produced for Alexandria by good local sculptors or whether it was made during an earlier dynasty and brought to Alexandria from elsewhere.

Whatever the answers to these questions, the presence of such a patently divine statue among the debris littering the southern coast of the royal port is a factor worthy of our attention. These are the remains of a statue that was brutally smashed, and which bears no sign of having been re-cut from an earlier architectural block. Such an idol could only have stood in a sanctuary of significant size and one dedicated to an Egyptian cult. Is it coincidence that it was found near the head of the colossus? No one can say.

Finally, no great distance away must have stood a third Pharaonic statue of enormous size, of which only the base and the front part of the left foot have been found. The inscription on the base reveals the name 'Merenptah' (c. 1213–1204 BC). Judging by the size of the fragment, the statue as a whole must have been gigantic.

The name 'Merenptah', inscribed on this statue base, gives us a clue regarding the identity of the figure.

All that remains of the colossus are these five enormous toes.

A typically Egyptian creation, combining a falcon's head with a human ear, a Pharaonic-style headdress and a lion's body (now missing).

123

The headdress indicates that the statue was that of a falcon-headed sphinx rather than a straightforward representation of a falcon.

This drawing was done by hand underwater and shows the creature's human ear very clearly. The ear is the attribute of the gods who 'listen' to human prayers. It is also a valuable clue as to the statue's date, suggesting (in accordance with similar imagery) that the sculpture could not have been executed prior to the 7th century BC.

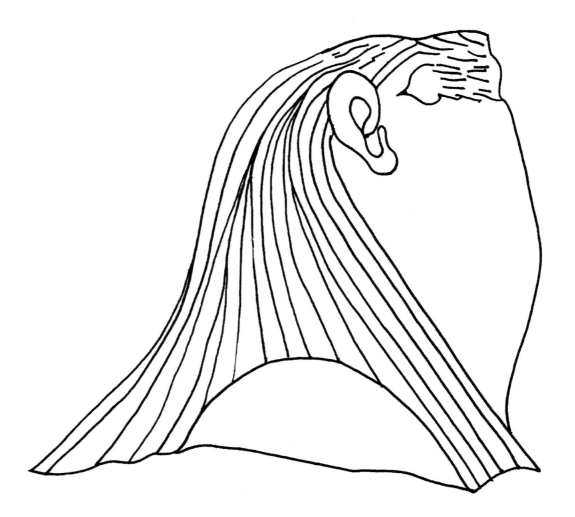

There are comparisons to be drawn between the Alexandrian falcon and the hieracosphinx, or hawk-headed sphinx, representing Amenhotep II, as seen in the tomb of Qenamon (large drawing), or the one representing Horus-Hekenon, in the naos at Saft (small drawing).

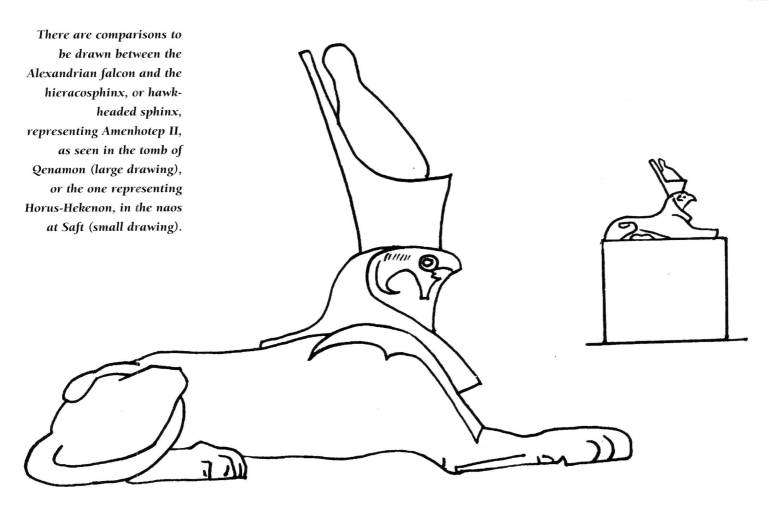

The gigantic size of the falcon head is clear from this picture (where it dwarfs the diver's face): the entire statue must have measured some 4.5m.

There are days when archaeology seems rather like a detective inquiry. There was a mystery surrounding these stones and their hieroglyphic inscriptions: clearly part of the same structure, they were nevertheless discovered tens of metres apart...

Mysterious hieroglyphs

Our exploration of the ancient coastline was to present us with a puzzle which left us temporarily perplexed. Where a block of stone is engraved with an inscription it is possible to systematically take an impression or produce a drawing of it and so decipher the inscription much more readily. Now, after carefully examining five fragments of pink granite with similar characteristics, we realised that two of them matched and, together, formed a single large sculpted stone 1.5m high. There was nothing surprising perhaps in the fact that two pieces of the giant puzzle should fit together – except that one of these fragments was found on the coast and the other in the middle of the island. How was this dispersal to be explained? We took the liberty of shifting the coastal fragment, with the help of buoys, and setting it on top of the base, then taking an impression of the whole thing before putting the block back *in situ*. By analysing the inscriptions we were then able to shed some light on the matter.

Although they had ended up in different places (two on the island, three on the southern coast of the royal harbour), these five architectural elements originally belonged to the same monument, which analysis of the inscriptions enabled us to date to the reign of Apries (589–570 BC), king of the 26th (Saitic) Dynasty. The general shape and the proportions of all of them are still recognisable despite the presence of fractures and larger cracks, visibly secondary accidents which have disfigured the blocks. A reference on one of them to Atoum confirms the general hypothesis that the architectural elements of the earliest dynasties were imported from Heliopolis. The allusion to the gods of Kher-Aha further supports this hypothesis: Kher-Aha, situated on the site where Old Cairo now stands and known to the Greeks as the Babylon of Egypt, was an administrative dependency of Heliopolis, and had close religious ties with the temple of Ra. The Heliopolitan origin of the five fragments raises the possibility that a block of pink granite discovered on the submerged site of Qait-Bey may also have come from the same construction by Apries. Engraved on the block is an inscription naming *the lord of the Apries arm, loved by the Powers of Heliopolis*. Apries' monumental building works in the temples of Heliopolis are well documented, and the autobiography inscribed by his chief steward Peftaouneit on the statue which he placed in the temple of Atoum offers an indication of their importance.

So what happened? The huge monoliths once stood – perhaps in a hall of pillars or serving as an architrave to a door – in a building in Heliopolis embellished during the reign of Apries; they were then removed and deposited, possibly re-erected, in a temple in Alexandria. At an unspecified date they were cut up and re-used as materials in some new construction, the stone from which was itself probably used during a reconstruction project in Roman or Byzantine times, for the benefit of several new buildings.

The case is typical of the strange vagaries to which such architectural elements were exposed, the way they were repeatedly displaced, recycled and mistreated. It is this kind of thing that makes our work so difficult and so intriguing.

The reassembled block after the coastal fragment was moved – not without some difficulty – and placed on top of its twin, lying at the centre of the island. It was an extraordinary moment when the two inscriptions were put together – and two pieces of the giant puzzle finally fell into place.

The peninsula

*Situated between Alexandria's two largest docks, the peninsula occupies a strategic position
and provided an excellent choice for the construction of harbour facilities. When we set out to sketch the
plans of the famous Timonium and the temple dedicated to Poseidon, from whom the peninsula takes its
name, we still had a number of pleasant surprises in store.*

**Disc-shaped lead ingots. Some were piled up
on the paved area of the jetty; others had slid
down the slope.**

Small pink granite capital on the peninsula.

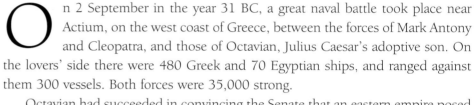

On 2 September in the year 31 BC, a great naval battle took place near Actium, on the west coast of Greece, between the forces of Mark Antony and Cleopatra, and those of Octavian, Julius Caesar's adoptive son. On the lovers' side there were 480 Greek and 70 Egyptian ships, and ranged against them 300 vessels. Both forces were 35,000 strong.

Octavian had succeeded in convincing the Senate that an eastern empire posed a genuine and imminent threat to Rome, and on these grounds had declared war on Cleopatra. The battle was a turning point. Antony was defeated and the civil wars that had followed the assassination of Julius Caesar were finally brought to an end.

Seeing himself abandoned by his many followers, after the defeat at Actium, Strabo tells us, *Antony retired to Alexandria and resolved to spend the rest of his days leading the solitary life of Timon,* and to that effect he had a palace built in a remote corner of the bay. It was long thought that this palace, known as the Timonium, was situated at the end of a long breakwater on the actual site of the island of Antirhodos, which itself was erroneously located at the seaward extremity of the peninsula. Since the precise topography of the area has been established, we know that the palace in fact stood at the far end of the mole, in the south-west of the peninsula, on what Strabo describes as *a kind of elbow jutting out into the sea.*

The general topography

The peninsula is 350m long and 150m wide. A series of imposing quays, now badly damaged, were constructed, using limestones and mortar, on its north-eastern side. There are four port constructions: near the base, on the north-eastern side, a small jetty measuring 40m x 6m, constructed of large limestone blocks and covered with paving stones; further to the north-east, a jetty measuring 50m x 7m, constructed of horizontal layers of 10cm x 10cm limestone blocks embedded in lime mortar, with an additional leg 12m long jutting out at an angle from the first; at the north-eastern extremity an impressive breakwater measuring 180m x 18m, in good condition despite some sagging in a few areas; and finally a substantial mole extending to the south-east, measuring 90m x 25m and covered in a limestone paving in a good state of repair. This mole terminates in a paved esplanade, 50m x 20m, and it was here that the famous Timonium stood.

The esplanade is in fact strewn with limestone blocks of varying sizes and large lumps of ancient mortar (measuring up to 3.5m in thickness), while lower down red granite column shafts, 90cm in diameter, lie alongside marble and quartzite elements. In addition to the subfoundations dating from the 1st century BC, excavations carried out on the site of the Timonium have also revealed reconstructions dating from the period of the Antonines (2nd century AD). The majority of the harbour structures appear to have been adapted in fact to the fashion of that period, as is demonstrated by carbon dating and dendrochronological analysis of all the wooden subfoundation structures in various parts of Alexandria's eastern harbour. Examination of the commonplace objects found on site (gold jewellery, oil lamps, small amphorae, items dating from the time of Antoninus Pius) confirm these different dates.

The other sector where the archaeological remains are particularly dense is the base of the peninsula, where two concentrations of broken red granite columns on paved areas have been found, one in the north, the other in the south. It was here that a temple stood, some remnants of whose treasure (such as gold jewellery) have been discovered. Was this the temple dedicated to Poseidon, god of the sea? One of the most powerful gods in the Greek pantheon, Poseidon was the object of particular veneration in the maritime city of Alexandria, and a statue of him is said to have adorned the lighthouse.

As well as architectural elements belonging to these two great buildings a number of other remarkable finds are worth noting. These include sections of wall constructed of flat bricks joined with mortar, fragments of sarcophagi, circular lead ingots, a decapitated sphinx and, most importantly, a block carrying hieroglyphic inscriptions on three sides, as well as the disturbingly beautiful head of a statue.

Wooden posts like these (now detached from the sea-bed) were used to reinforce the floor of the peninsula in the vicinity of any structures that were erected.

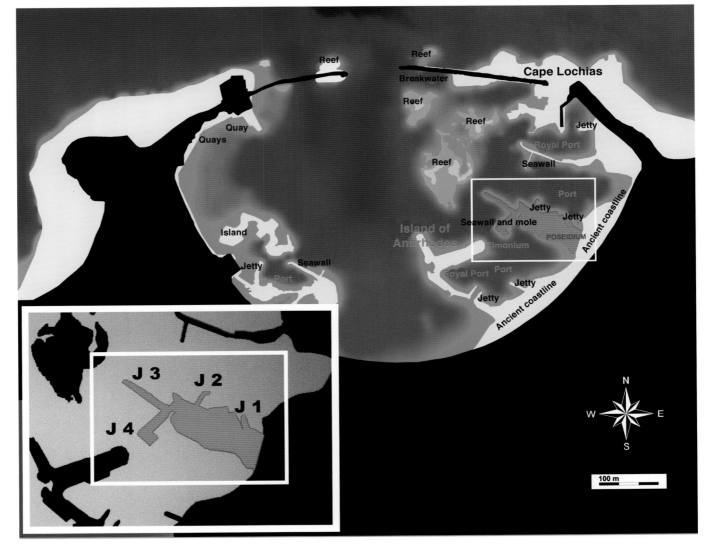

The Portus Magnus, with the peninsula shown in red. The inset reveals the location of the various jetties.
J 1 : jetty n° 1 where the lead ingots were discovered.
J 2 : jetty n° 2, in an excellent state of repair.
J 3 : the Poseidium peninsula's main jetty.
J 4 : jetty leading to the esplanade on which the Timonium was located.

Blocks bearing hieroglyphic inscriptions were found on the peninsula – for the inquisitive reader there follows an account of how we deciphered and interpreted them.

Reading the hieroglyphs

To the archaeologist exploring the hazy world of the ocean bed, the discovery of a block of sculpted granite is a source of huge excitement; but to come across a block engraved with hieroglyphs is a piece of fortune beyond his wildest dreams, promising as it does the unfolding of some marvellous story. This particular story was three pages long (the marks on the fourth side of the block having totally disappeared): three pages of inscriptions which were cleaned and then moulded so that they could be passed on to the epigraphers.

The block was identified as a section of an obelisk dedicated to Seti I. It is 0.55m tall, approximately 2m wide and 0.7m deep.

The course of Seti's life was an extraordinary one. Although he was not born into the ruling family and not therefore in line to become king, he reigned from *circa* 1291 BC to 1279 BC, and fathered no less a son than the great Rameses II himself. The throne of Horus was previously occupied by Horemheb, the last king of the 18th Dynasty, who, finding himself without a male heir, identified a worthy successor, one who was both intelligent and determined, in the person of the young Seti, son of his high official. The king was crafty, however: knowing that the court and the priesthood would oppose the nomination of a young man with such brilliant credentials, he handed over power to his old official, Rameses I, whom his opponents were confident of manipulating. And two years later, on the death of Rameses I, Seti took control as planned.

He proved to be a moderate and wise administrator and an enlightened sovereign, who succeeded in obliterating from memory the excesses of his predecessors. In his eagerness to restore the royal image in all its glory, Seti also made a name for himself as a great builder. Numerous sanctuaries bear his cartouche, evidence that he had set himself the task of either restoring or embellishing them, and it is to Seti I that we owe some of ancient Egypt's most stunning buildings, notably the hypostyle hall in the great temple of Amon at Karnak.

The obelisk at Alexandria is also dedicated to Amon, represented on face A, or, more precisely, to the sun god in his multiple forms. On face B the god Ptah is shown in his sanctuary and face C features Atoum, a god with a human face wearing a solar disc on his head. The designation Atoum is not often found, and this representation of the god with the solar disc is even less common: he is most frequently depicted wearing the *pschent* (the white and red double crown symbolising power over the two united kingdoms of Egypt).

These three pictures therefore invoke three of the four primary gods of the Rameside state: Amon of Thebes, the Heliopolitan sun in the form of Atum-Khepri, and Ptah of Memphis. We may suppose that the fourth would have been Set, another form of the sun, particularly dear to Seti's family since their name derives from his. The monument's fourth face probably suffered the same fate as those innumerable other monuments representing the god Set which were hammered flat towards the 8th century BC, when the Osirian myth became so popular that Set, the rival of Osiris, fell into disgrace. Images of Set were either destroyed or transformed by slicing off his large ears and endowing him instead with horns, attributes of the illustrious Amon. This mutilation was so widespread that the rare representations of Set that still exist can most often be explained as sculptural elements that have been re-used in locations where the image was no longer visible. In all probability, the obelisk found at Alexandria (re-using a monument a great deal older than the city itself) was a victim of the same severe proscription as those countless other images of Set.

BLOCK DB4 N° 747

Peninsula
Grey granite
Lat. : 31° 12' 3863 N
Long. : 29° 54' 2023 E
Depth: 4.8m.

E

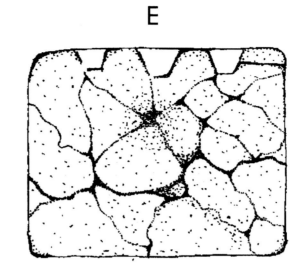

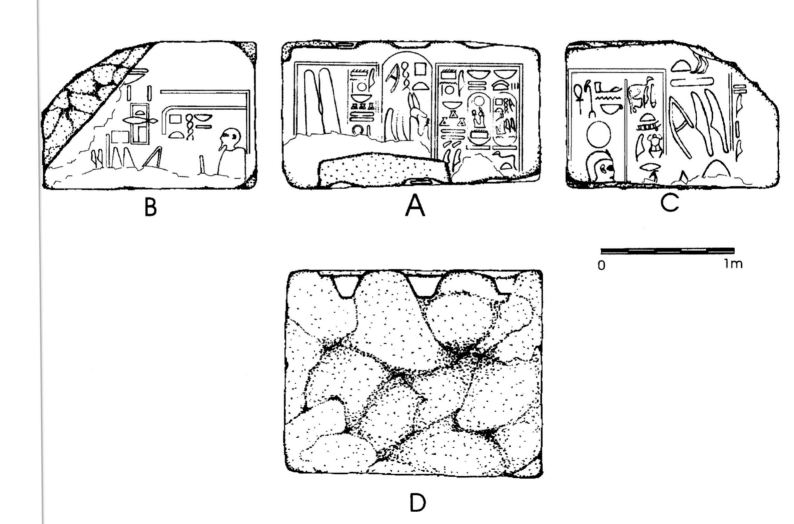

B

A

C

D

Face A of the obelisk: the inscription can be read more easily on the obliquely lit moulding (below) than on the stone itself.

Inscribed in the central column is the name Seti-Merenptah. The left-hand cartouche reads: "Amon-Re, lord of the Thrones of the Two Lands" and the right-hand one: "The lord of the Two Lands, Menmare, the lord of the crowns, Seti-Merenptah, beloved of Amon-Re, lord of the Thrones of the Two Lands."

Face B (above and below) is damaged, but the image of the god, seen in profile, in his sanctuary is still clearly visible on the right.

The central column reads "beloved of the lords of the Great House." On the left, all that remains is the qualifier "beloved of [Ptah in] Heliopolis;" on the right: "Ptah, lord of Maat."

On face C, the solar disc can clearly be seen on the left, worn as a headdress by the god Atoum (depicted with human features).

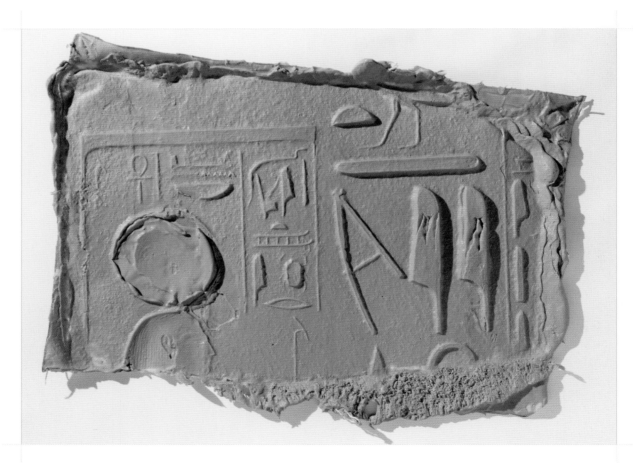

The central column signifies: "beloved of [Re-Hor]akhti, endowed with life…" On the left, we read: "Words spoken by Atum-Khepri: I give you life." On the right, all that is legible is the qualifier "beloved of Atum-Khepri, the great god."

The beautiful Antonia Minor

Another find on the peninsula, one so magical that we might do better to speak of an apparition rather than a find, is the badly eroded white marble head of a woman. The head has been obliquely broken off at the base of the neck, and its features are blurred but gentle, its eyes only a faint evocation of what they must once have been.

Hairstyles are always a precious clue regarding identity and aesthetic trends, but in this case the style is difficult to distinguish. The woman's hair is parted in the middle of her forehead and forms a mass of sinuous waves falling either side of her face and joined together at an oblique angle on the nape of her neck, either coiled, braided or tied back in a bunch. Although imprecise, this arrangement of the hair appears on coins bearing the likeness of Antonia Minor (born in 37 BC), the daughter of Octavia and Mark Antony and mother of Germanicus and Claudius. The oval shape of her face and her pointed chin are further details that confirm the hypothesis, since this is how the princess is depicted in all other portraits of her.

Antonia Minor's hairstyle launched a fashion which was widely followed in private portraiture, and is even found on a head at Ephesus, capital of the Roman province of Asia Minor. The size of the Alexandrian sculpture, however, being slightly greater than life-size (35cm high), leads us to suppose that this is indeed an official portrait of the princess, who was honoured throughout the Roman Empire from the time of Tiberius, her brother-in-law, until the reign of her son Claudius.

This strangely beautiful statue, newly recovered from the sea, will win Antonia Minor a fresh set of admirers in centuries to come.

An exquisite female head in white marble. The face is badly eroded (though all the more magical for that) and difficult to identify, but the hairstyle provides valuable clues, indicating that the woman in question is probably Antonia Minor, mother of the Emperor Claudius.

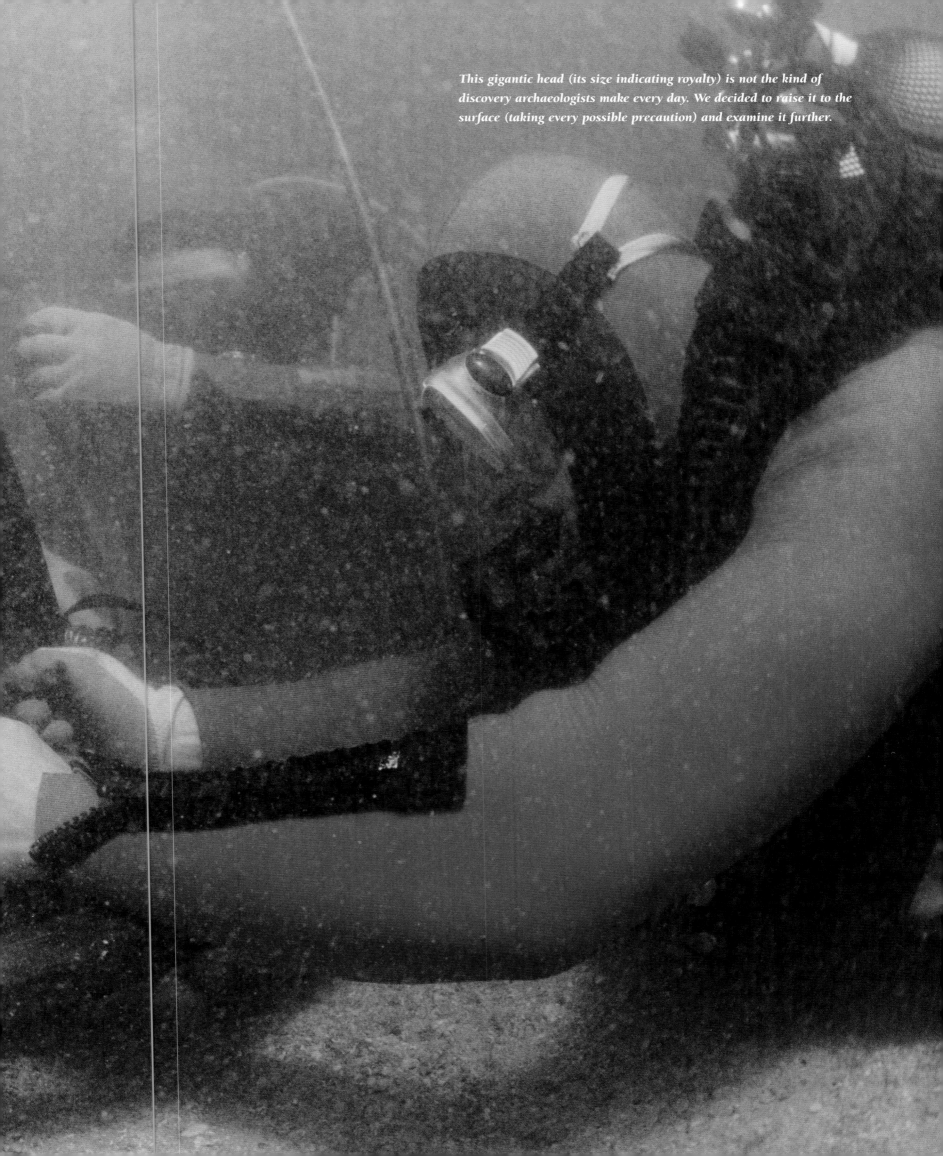

This gigantic head (its size indicating royalty) is not the kind of discovery archaeologists make every day. We decided to raise it to the surface (taking every possible precaution) and examine it further.

The Timonium

Some royal monuments are built as showpieces — somewhere to receive and entertain in magnificent style. The Timonium, by contrast, was a private retreat, constructed at the end of a breakwater that was itself an extension of the peninsula. It was here that Mark Antony sought to drown the bitterness of his military defeat, with only the sea for company.

The form of the Latin word Timonium tells us straightaway that it relates to a Roman building bearing the name of a certain Timon. Strabo confirms this meaning of the word when he describes the buildings that can be seen from the Portus Magnus. After pointing out the buildings constructed on Cape Lochias, then the small island of Antirhodos, he writes: *Beyond is the theatre, then the Poseidium, a kind of elbow jutting out into the sea, starting from what is known as the* Emporion *[the marketplace] and upon which a temple of Neptune [Poseidon] is built. Antony extended this elbow into the middle of the harbour, by means of a causeway, and at the end of it he constructed a palace, which he called the Timonium: this was the last thing he did when, seeing himself abandoned by his many supporters after the defeat at Actium, he retired to Alexandria and resolved to lead the solitary life of Timon for the rest of his days.*

A solitary city misanthrope

Timon of Athens was a famous misanthrope who lived at the time of the Peloponnesian War (431–404 BC). Aristophanes refers to him in *The Birds* (l. 1549), where Prometheus describes himself as *a Timon through and through*. In *Lysistrata* (l. 805–820) the female chorus address the chorus of old men with the following words: *There was a certain Timon, a descendant of Erinys who had no abode of his own and was hidden from view by the numerous spines that surrounded him. Now this Timon withdrew from the world, out of hatred, after liberally cursing the wickedness of men. So it was that, in opposition to yourselves, he nursed an immovable hatred for base men, although women enjoyed his good will.* Lucian wrote a dialogue, *Timon the misanthrope*, and the character of Timon is also the subject of a play by Shakespeare, *Timon of Athens*. Plutarch (*Life of Antony*, 69) devotes a chapter to him, quoting some of the bitter remarks he is reputed to have made. While tenderly embracing Alcibiades – who defected to the Spartans during the Peloponnesian War – Timon declared that he loved this young man because he knew that he would do the Athenians a great deal of harm. One day from the assembly platform he advised his audience that he was going to cut down a fig tree, but that anyone who wished could go and hang themselves before the tree was felled. Timon was buried at Halai, near the sea, where a rock fall rendered his tomb inaccessible. His epitaph, which he is said to have composed himself, read: *I rest here, my spirit crushed by an oppressive fate. You will never know my name. May you miserable wretches perish miserably!* A different version is quoted by the Greek poet Callimachus: *I, Timon the Misanthrope, dwell here. Go! Go away, cursing me all you wish; just go away!* An epigram from the *Palatine Anthology* (7, 317) imagines this dialogue with a passer-by: *Timon, you are no longer; so which do you hate, the light or the shade? – The shade, for in Hades you are more numerous still.*

Gold coin from the Antonine period, found on the site of the Timonium.

Childish amusements

Thanks to the underwater excavations carried out by Franck Goddio and his team in the eastern harbour, we are now able to locate the site of the Timonium, and will say more about this later when we come to study the harbours.

According to Roman propaganda, Antony's extravagant lifestyle was the adoption of an 'inimitable life', unworthy of a Roman, but utterly typical of the Orientals. Cleopatra organised receptions and entertainments that sometimes had a silly, childish side to them, and she and Antony laid on banquets and lavish parties for one another, developing what Antony's detractors might have described as an inimitable partnership in crime. One day when they were out fishing together, in an effort to impress Cleopatra, Antony asked a diver to swim up and secretly attach a large fish to his hook. Cleopatra, who enjoyed playing tricks on her lover, pretended to be taken in, but when they went out fishing again, she had a dried fish from the Black Sea, or the Euxine Sea as it was known, attached to Antony's hook, declaring: *General, leave us who reign over Pharos and Canopus our own line: cities, kingdoms and continents are what you catch.* The queen diced, drank, hunted and attended military reviews. Sometimes she disguised herself as a maidservant and, with Antony similarly dressed, went knocking on people's doors and making fun of them. Despite an occasionally violent reception, the couple continued to keep their identity a secret. According to Plutarch, *the Alexandrians enjoyed this buffoonery and took part in her games (which they relished) with a certain style and finesse. They said that Antony played a tragic role with the Romans and a comic one with them.* Laughter in Egypt, and in Alexandria in particular, was an integral component of social life. The French poet Henri Michaux grasped this form of wit perfectly, describing it as 'apotropaic', a means of warding off unhappiness or, at any rate, tragedy, and if we want to understand Alexandria we need to take this way of thinking and feeling into account. Behind their façades, freshly repainted thanks to the efforts of the city governor, the Alexandrians had to contend with life's difficulties; but an atmosphere of good humour nevertheless reigned in the city, and any traveller inclined to enquire too closely would simply be rewarded by a smile from passers-by.

Silver denarius bearing the head of Mark Antony.
© The British Museum

Obverse of the same coin, showing Cleopatra VII (as not quite the beauty we imagine). © The British Museum

Remains of the Timonium. Limestone construction blocks belonging to the foundations.

Collapsed columns at the base of the esplanade that originally supported the Timonium. These columns have tumbled down the sloping surface of the platform constructed from large blocks of mortar.

Piles and sheet-pile wall used to reinforce the esplanade on which the Timonium was built. Samples of wood taken from these remains have been carbon dated to 25 BC ± 45 years. Each pile is given a code, which is recorded on a label.

The foundations of the Timonium, uncovered for the first time. A graduated measuring rule, divided into 10cm segments, gives an idea of the scale.

The Poseidium

When the three sons of Cronos divided up the universe, Zeus inherited the sky, Hades the underworld and Poseidon the sea, while the earth remained common property. Poseidon is consequently one of the most powerful of the Greek gods, and the most feared by a seafaring people like the Alexandrians.

Aseaport like Alexandria could not have existed without a sanctuary dedicated to Poseidon, god of the sea. The only surviving reference to the sanctuary is from Strabo, when he lists the buildings that confront the visitor on entering the Portus Magnus. After mentioning the island of Antirhodos, he writes: *Beyond is the theatre, then the Poseidium, a kind of elbow jutting out into the sea, starting from what is known as the* Emporion [the marketplace] *and upon which a temple of Neptune [Poseidon] is built.* We may gather from the reference to the sanctuary – which Strabo locates but does not describe – that the sailors of Alexandria looked to the god of the sea for protection; but why should they need it?

A beautiful gold ring found on the site of the Poseidium.

The cruel sea

The Greeks and the Romans were great seafaring peoples and depended for their livelihood on fishing and maritime expeditions, and yet it would be wrong to suppose that they had no fear of the sea. For the people of Alexandria the sea presented a particular set of perils, being 'closed' to them from October until the spring, during which time sailing was suspended.

The image of the good pilot was commonly applied to the head of state who knew how to 'steer his ship'. And Greek theatre (to cite but one source of evidence) is littered with references to the sea as a thing that inspires fear. For Aeschylus the sea is the image of misfortune. The wanderings of Io, ancestor of the Egyptians, are marked by a horror of it: in *Prometheus Bound* Io fails to cross the Black Sea and in *Suppliant Women* she reaches Egypt only by hugging the coasts of Greece and then of Asia Minor and Phoenicia.

Sophocles used analogies borrowed from the sea and its milieu almost exclusively to depict the misfortune of either the individual or the city. The seas bordering Thrace and Crete and the Euxine Sea are singled out as being especially dangerous. Philoctetes, a hero of the Trojan War, says to his companions: *Let us pray to the nymphs of the sea to ensure our safe return.* The Alexandrians offered this prayer to Poseidon.

In Euripides' *Trojan Women* Athena and Poseidon decide to punish the Greeks on their return from Troy by afflicting them with calamitous storms at sea. It was as well to stay on good terms with a god as touchy as Poseidon, which is why he had his own temple in Alexandria.

Poseidon as protector

The god of the sea is portrayed on numerous Alexandrian coins, which can be studied in the catalogue of the Dattari Collection *Numi Augg Alexandrini* and in *Sylloge Nummorum Graecorum*.

The coins sometimes show him wearing a *himation* (cloak) and holding a trident, or else naked, standing on a *biga* (two-horse chariot) drawn by seahorses running over the waves, with a trident in his left hand and a dolphin in his right; or again standing, naked, holding his trident upright in his left hand, a dolphin in his right, his foot planted on the prow of a ship. Sometimes just his head and shoulders are shown, from the right side, with a band encircling his head. He is also to be found standing, with the *himation* over his shoulders, holding his trident in his left hand, and a *patera* (round sacrificial dish) on a lighted altar in his right; or again full-length, naked, with his crown on the left side of his head, his foot planted on a dolphin, and something resembling an ear of grain in his right hand, his trident in his left, and a palm branch behind him. The Alexandrians exhibited remarkable freedom and independence from classical iconographic conventions, and one is struck simultaneously by the diversity of these images and by the permanence of the Alexandrian symbols.

The series studied by Soheir Bakhoum, dating from the time of Augustus and Trajan, include a coin bearing on the reverse Poseidon in a *biga* drawn by seahorses and several coins showing the bearded head of Poseidon Isthmios encircled with a band inscribed with the letters of the god's name.

As Michel Amandry, curator at the Bibliothèque nationale in Paris, explains, Alexandrian coinage was used in a closed-circuit system. Coins minted in Alexandria remained within the confines of Egypt, and coins minted in the rest of the Mediterranean region never entered Egypt. The system originated with Ptolemy I, who closed his borders to foreign currency in 305 BC. When the Romans took control of Egypt in 30 BC, they decided to retain the system, which represented an important source of fiscal profits.

Poseidon has his place in the repertory of Alexandrian coins, but he is not alone. The coinage reflects Egyptian religion and culture, which is why we also encounter images of Serapis and Hermanoubis or Hippocrates, and sacred animals like the crocodile, the Apis bull and the serpent Agathodaimon. Images appearing on the reverse of the coins include, *inter alia*, the lighthouse at Alexandria and the Serapeum – useful contributions to our knowledge of Egyptian monuments – but unfortunately not the Poseidium.

Silver tetradrachma from the reign of Demetrius Poliorcetes showing Poseidon carrying a trident. © The British Museum

Obverse of the same coin showing Victory at the prow of a ship. © The British Museum

Excavations on the Poseidium peninsula

The remains of a large monument have been discovered at the base of the peninsula. Rather than belonging to the temple seen by Strabo, these appear in fact to correspond to a later reconstruction dating from Roman times.

Numerous limestone blocks are scattered around a large rectangular area built of mortar whose datable reinforcing points to the Antonine period (138–192 AD), while sections of pink granite columns lying to the south-west illustrate the effects of the cataclysm which destroyed the monument.

An electronic map (below) of the temple site, situated at the base of the peninsula, shows the remains of the great monument on a bathymetric background where the red areas indicate the shallowest levels and the blue the deepest. The yellow squares mark the location of the limestone blocks and the pink lozenges that of the pink granite column shafts. The large rectangular space at the centre of the limestone blocks corresponds to the solid masses of ancient mortar, 1m thick, which constituted the foundations of the monument. The temple precincts were reinforced with wooden piles.

Electronic map of the remains of a large monument situated at the base of the Poseidium peninsula.

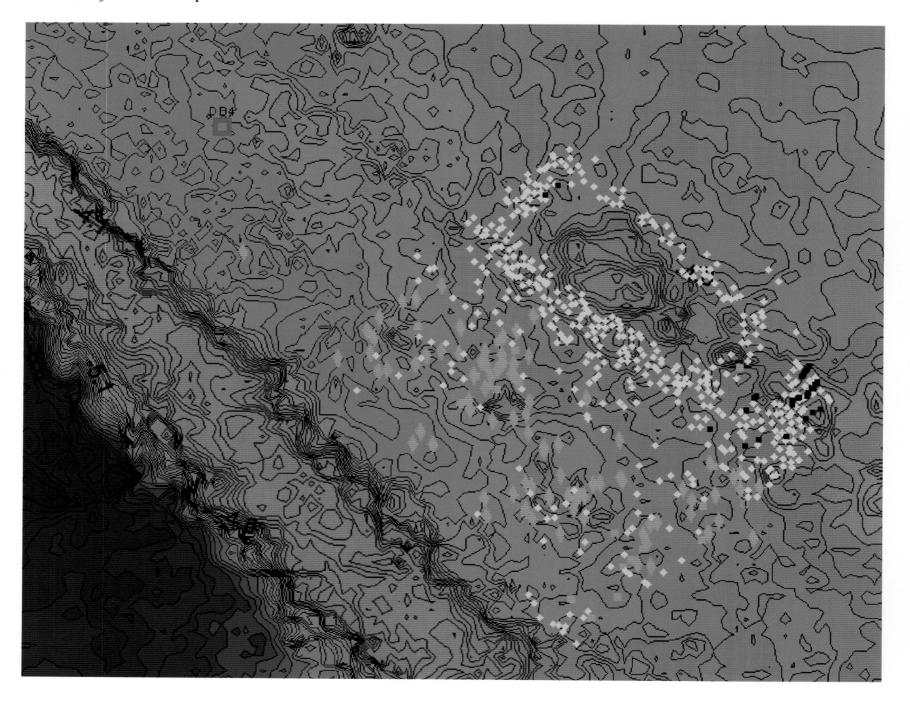

One of the rows of piles used to reinforce the mortar foundations of the large monument on the Poseidium peninsula. The piles are spaced 30cm apart.

Diver measuring the piles used to reinforce the ground around the Poseidium monument.

The ports

This city facing the open sea was a great centre of commerce. Known as Rome's granary, it relied upon the export of cereals and the import of materials which were in short supply locally, most notably wood. Many ships were built here too, the shipyards occupying the whole of the westernmost area of the Portus Magnus. Alexandria was the city of ports – commercial ports, royal ports, private ports, ports for the use of galleys and for the passage of goods and people.

Although we generally use the singular to describe a city as a seaport, where Alexandria is concerned we are obliged to speak in the plural, since this particular city boasted a number of harbours or ports, all of them quite different from one another.

Word games

Alexandria's eastern harbour was called the Great Harbour – Megas Limin in Greek or Portus Magnus in Latin. Its western harbour was situated on the other side of the mole known as the Heptastadion and was styled Eunostos, the 'port of safe return', although in fact it was difficult to access due to the presence of shoals and barrier reefs and the prevailing winds blowing from the north-west. This use of antiphrasis is common in Greek: the Black Sea, which was extremely perilous, having relatively few safe anchorage sites and hostile inhabitants populating its shores, was nevertheless called the Euxine, or 'hospitable', sea.

The name Antirhodos can be interpreted in two different ways. According to Jean Yoyotte and Pascal Charvet in their commentary to *Voyage en Égypte de Strabon*, "As a result of its name, the little island of Antirhodos would have represented a challenge to a stubbornly independent city-state (before it became an ally of Rome), whose merchants, engineers and intellectuals rivalled those of the Alexandrian monarchy." Antirhodos can also be understood quite simply as 'the Rhodes opposite', since Alexandria was in the southern Mediterranean, while Rhodes was in the north.

In the western harbour there was an artificial basin which was given the name Kibotos (the 'coffer') on account of its enclosed position at the foot of Rhakotis Hill. Within the eastern part of the Portus Magnus, the underwater excavations carried out by Franck Goddio and his team (and described in his book *Alexandria: the submerged royal quarters*) have revealed the existence of three interior ports, as indicated by the overall plan on p. 149. His recent excavations in the western part of the Portus Magnus have also revealed a large additional port with several docks, situated just opposite the Heptastadion, the huge causeway which connected the coast to the island of Pharos. It appears that the latter served as a transit area between the eastern and western harbours (cf. *The* navalia, p. 156). This configuration was completed by a series of substantial moles constructed along the length of the island of Pharos.

Portus Magnus

Map of the Portus Magnus incorporating the submerged regions of the ancient city dating back to Roman times.

Communication between the eastern and western harbours

The Eunostos was not just a sea harbour but also a river port, into which the Mahmoudieh canal flowed. Known in antiquity as the 'guardian spirit', this canal branched off the Canopic arm of the Nile, bringing water from the river to the city and also serving as a route for the conveyance of products from the delta. For Alexandria to be, as Strabo called it, the *Emporion* or marketplace of the ancient world, there needed to be some means of communication between the two harbours to enable the transhipment of cargo. These transhipments were facilitated by the grid layout based on the Hippodamian model and entrusted to the celebrated architect Deinocrates: thanks to Alexandria's straight roads carts could travel by the most direct route and did not have to contend with dangerous bends.

According to Strabo, this layout also favoured the circulation of air through the city, particularly when the summer winds were blowing, from which he concluded: *So summer is a very agreeable season for the Alexandrians*. It was for this same reason that ministers moved their offices and archives from Cairo to Alexandria for the summer season during the reign of King Farouk (1936–52). After spending several summers in Alexandria, however, it is possible to feel less enthusiastic than Strabo, since in July and August these days the only place where one can breathe properly is on the coast road.

Was it the best choice of site on which to construct a capital? This was a question that was debated by the two great philosophers of antiquity, Plato and Aristotle.

Why fear the sea?

For Plato, building a city on the edge of the sea entailed grave dangers. Firstly, it risked introducing corruption into the city, tainting the values of a population reliant on the hinterland and agriculture by exposing it to international trade. Secondly, it could inflate the population and promote a spirit of anarchy, more especially as merchants and sailors were undesirable additions to the city. Finally, as Plato saw it, the quality of bravery declined in direct proportion to a nation's reliance on ships. He considered that the naval victories won by the Athenians at Salamis and Cape Artemision in 480 BC had turned the Greeks into cowards, whereas the land battles at Marathon (490 BC) and Plataea (479 BC) had created better men united by a greater sense of solidarity.

Taking the opposite view from his master (as was to be expected), Aristotle judged that a nation needed to be able to defend itself both at sea and on land. For the sake of importing and exporting goods, moreover, it had to open itself up to outside trade, and this in turn required the development of its fleet. As for the risk of overpopulation, this could be avoided if sailors were not assimilated into the city and the length of their stay was carefully controlled. If a city was open to the sea, there was no need to enclose it behind high walls. A city needed, on the one hand, to be in communication with every part of its territory; on the other, to be able to offer transport facilities so that products from the soil, wood and construction materials could be brought in.

As Alexander's tutor, Aristotle had expounded these theories to him at length, and Alexander was astute enough to recognise the merits of Aristotle's arguments.

And so the city of Alexandria was born.

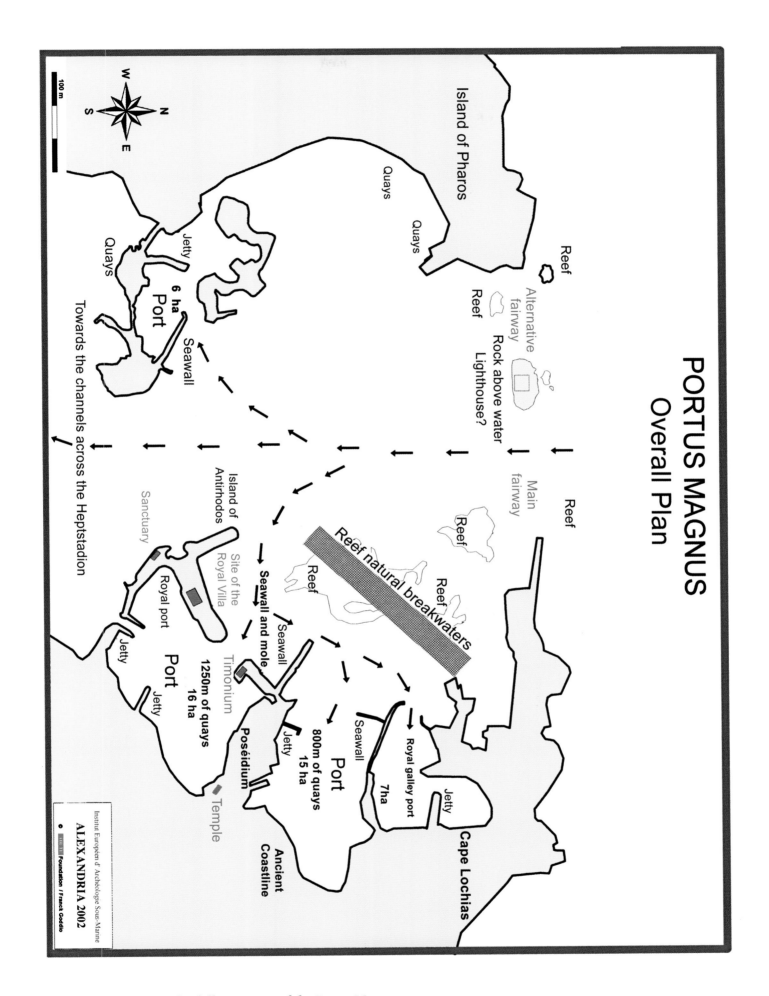

PORTUS MAGNUS
Overall Plan

Island of Pharos

Quays

Quays

Reef

Reef

Alternative
fairway

Rock above water
Lighthouse?

Reef

Main
fairway

Reef

Reef

Reef

Reef natural breakwaters

Reef

Quays

Jetty

6 ha
Port

Seawall

Quays

Towards the channels across the Heptstadion

Sanctuary

Island of
Antirhodos

Site of the
Royal Villa

Royal port

Jetty

Jetty

Port

1250m of quays
16 ha

Timonium

Seawall and mole

Seawall

Jetty

Poséidium

Temple

Port
800m of quays
15 ha

Seawall

Jetty

7ha

Royal galley port

Jetty

Cape Lochias

Ancient
Coastline

100 m

W N S E

Institut Européen d'Archéologie Sous-Marine

ALEXANDRIA 2002

Foundation / Franck Goddio

Map showing access to the different ports of the Portus Magnus.

Alexandria's modern fishing port occupies the site of the ancient navalia and the Pharos docks.

The royal ports from the point of view of a 20th-century engineer

According to the maritime engineer, Arthur de Graauw, of SOGREAH Engineering, based in Grenoble, France, the expert in harbour installations is primarily interested in the following:

- **Overall plan** The configuration of a harbour depends on navigation conditions (winds, waves) and the types of ships using it (sail- or oar-propelled). The size of the vessels determines the degree of acceptable turbulence and the decision whether or not to construct a breakwater to serve as a storm barrier. The length of the quays is determined by the number of vessels using the harbour.
- **Harbour structures** The water depth at the quayside, and consequently the height and structure of the quay, depend on the draught of the vessels using the harbour. The materials locally available (wood, stone, mortar) together with methods of construction influence the structures specific to a particular region and time.

Cross-section diagram of an ancient quay.

Overall plan

Let us start by considering two factors that affect all vessels: wind and waves. We can reasonably assume that wind and wave conditions have not altered, or at least not much, since antiquity. Current statistics demonstrate that the prevailing winds (and waves) off the coast of Alexandria are west to northerly (more than 50% of the time as a yearly average and 70–90% of the time from June to September). A second important directional sector is the north to easterly (20–30% of the time from October to May) – a significant consideration in Alexandria since it was the reason for choosing a double harbour.

The construction of a double harbour was motivated by the presence of two principal wind and wave directions. Where such circumstances exist, as they not uncommonly do, it is an advantage to be able to move ships from one anchorage to another in order to gain optimum protection in all weather and sea conditions. Once the

Heptastadion had been built, the island of Pharos became a peninsula which met this criterion perfectly:

- to the west lay the Eunostos harbour,
- to the east lay the Portus Magnus.

And, thanks to the ingenious construction of channels intersecting the Heptastadion, ships could sail from one harbour to the other without venturing out to sea – although it is worth noting that the western section of the roads at Alexandria must have started gradually silting up following the construction of the Heptastadion for this strip of coastline to curve in the way it does today.

It must have seemed logical to construct the eastern harbour next to the Heptastadion, where it would have been protected by the island of Pharos – at the spot where fishermen shelter today from the predominant west to northerly winds. Whatever its technical merits, such an argument does not appear to have prevailed, since the three ports that have been located are actually on

the opposite side of the bay, adjacent to Cape Lochias (modern-day Cape Silsileh), where the royal palaces were situated. This eastern sector of the roads is relatively more exposed to the north-west swell, and it was for this reason that a breakwater was constructed to reinforce the natural barrier provided by the emerging reefs.

In order to gain access to the docks, ships had to negotiate their way round to the south and west of the reefs. This enabled them to enter the roads with the wind behind them before the sails were stowed; they were then rowed towards the north-east and proceeded into one of the three ports.

As regards the types of vessel which used the harbour, it has been possible to identify a few large commercial vessels, but we are in fact better informed about the naval fleets of the time. Not all the ships mentioned passed through the harbour at Alexandria, but they are included for the purposes of comparison.

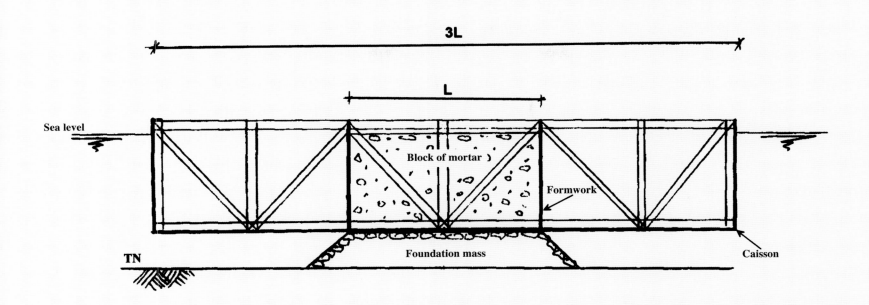

3L

L

Sea level

Block of mortar

Formwork

TN

Foundation mass

Caisson

Floating caisson.

During this time, when the Romans and Carthaginians were confronting one another in their triremes and quinqueremes in the western Mediterranean (at the decisive battle of the First Punic War off the Aegates Islands, 241 BC), the Macedonians and Alexandrians were constructing gigantic galleys. Some of these huge ships were still being built centuries later – Antony ranged a number of them against Octavian's fleet at the Battle of Actium (2 September 31 BC). The most assiduous of these ancient shipbuilders was undoubtedly Ptolemy II, who, at the time of his death in 246 BC, left a fleet of warships that included:

- 2 'thirties' (30 oarsmen a side);
- 1 'twenty';
- 4 'thirteens';
- 2 'twelves';
- 14 'elevens';
- 67 'nines' and 'sevens';
- 22 'sixes' and 'fives' (quinqueremes);
- 4 'threes' (triremes);
- 150 'twos' (biremes).

This makes a total of around 10 large vessels (measuring between 50 x 10m and 70 x 20m), 80 medium-sized vessels (45 x 8.5m) and 175 small vessels (between 20 x 2.5m and 35 x 5 m) – a fleet of some 265 ships.

This is similar to the number of warships we encounter during other periods. Pompey's fleet for his war against the pirates, waged between 67 and 66 BC, consisted of 200 quinqueremes and 30 triremes, and Antony's fleet for the battle of Actium was made up of 220 ships (his largest was a 'ten'). We also know that at other periods the Alexandrian fleet was less extensive. The fleet burned by Caesar at the Battle of Alexandria in 48 BC comprised 50 triremes and quinqueremes, 60 other vessels were beached in the arsenals.

As an exercise in imagining the overall plan of Alexandria's eastern harbour, we calculated how we might house Ptolemy II's entire fleet within the parameters of the three harbours.

The approximate surface area of each harbour is as follows:

- first harbour: 7 hectares;
- second harbour: 5 hectares with approximately 800m of quays;
- third harbour: 16 hectares with approximately 1,250m of quays.

We concluded that the first harbour could easily accommodate the 10 large vessels referred to above. The 80 mid-sized vessels and 25 small vessels could be lined up side by side, stern to quay in the second harbour, and the third harbour (with quay space for up to 250 quinqueremes) could house the remaining 150 small vessels.

By way of comparison, it is perhaps worth mentioning the dimensions of the other great harbours in antiquity.

- Piraeus at Athens
- Cantharus (commercial): 1,000 x 500m (50 hectares), 100 boatsheds;
- Zea (military): circular with a diameter of 300m (7 hectares), 196 boatsheds;
- Munychia: 82 boatsheds (approx. 5 hectares).
- Carthage
- Commercial harbour: 500 x 300m (15 hectares) in addition to the Lake of Tunis;
- Cothon (military): circular with a diameter of 330m and a central island (7 hectares of water), 220 boatsheds.
- Rome
- Portus: Porto Claudio (approx. 60 to 80 hectares) and Porto Trajano (33 hectares);
- Misenum (military): base of Octavian's imperial fleet for the battle of Actium;
- Puteoli (commercial): situated alongside Misenum in the Bay of Naples.

We can see from this that the Portus Magnus was of average size in relation to the other large harbours of the time.

Harbour structures

It is an irony of civilisation that the naval harbours of antiquity resembled the marinas of our own times in terms of their overall dimensions and the size of the ships using them (a luxury yacht measures between 15 and 70m or more). The ancient galleys had a shallower draught, however, in the order of 1 to 1.5m, although the largest ships must have had a draught that could reach 4m.

The two main types of harbour structures were breakwaters, which provided a barrier against the waves, and quays.

The breakwaters could be either sloping embankments of rough stone or vertical structures made of blocks. What remains of Alexandria's ancient breakwaters out to sea has not (as yet) been explored since the ancient structures are probably located beneath their modern counterparts.

The internal breakwaters which protected each of the three harbours consisted of a sloping embankment on the outer face and, in the majority of cases, a quay constructed from blocks of mortar on the structure's inner face.

The various structures can be classified as follows depending on which materials were used:

- wooden – wooden platforms supported by piles of stone pillars;
- without mortar – blocks of hewn stone, possibly with an infill between two facings;
- with mortar, without pozzolana (a porous volcanic ash used in making hydraulic cements) – massive blocks formed by pouring mortar into a wooden formwork in dry conditions;
- with mortar, with pozzolana – massive blocks formed by pouring mortar into a formwork underwater.

The technique using blocks of hewn stone is the oldest of these. For structures of a certain width, two separate facings were constructed using stone blocks and the cavity between them was filled with un-graded quarry materials. The surface this provided was then covered with paving. It was important that the blocks weighed no more than a tonne apiece so that they could be readily manoeuvred using the lift-ing devices available at the time. The blocks found at Tyr in the southern har-bour weigh around 500kg, although, to provide greater resilience, blocks weighing 10 tonnes or more were used in places exposed to the waves.

The mortar was made of slaked lime, sand and water. Since this mixture could only harden in the open air, and not underwater, the following mechanism was devised for use in marine construction work. A wooden formwork was installed in the water, at the site chosen for the construction of the quay, and filled with sand to just above the water level. The mortar was then poured on to this bed of sand and allowed to dry in the open air. In order to place the mortar in position on the sea-bed, the sand simply had to be emptied from the formwork by opening the doors let into its sides.

The introduction of pozzolana by the Romans in *circa* 30 BC revolutionised hydraulic construction work. This silico-aluminous material of volcanic origin combines with lime in the presence of water and enables mortar prepared in this way to harden underwater. The use of poz-zolana rendered obsolete the process described in the previous paragraph, since the mortar could now be poured directly into the formwork installed on the sea-bed. The Alexandrians had not yet acquired this expertise, however, at the time when the eastern harbour was constructed.

The large quay blocks discovered in Alexandria's third harbour (typically 5–8m wide, 10–15m long and 1–3m high) do not contain pozzolana and the dating of the wood indicates a period when pozzolana did not yet exist in Egypt (c. 250 BC). The presence of wood beneath the block indica-tes that the formwork almost certainly formed part of a floating caisson (a tech-nique also used at Caesarea under Herod and still in use today).

We may suppose that after being floated above the quay under construction, the caisson was weighted so that it sank down to the sea-bed, where a foundation surface had been prepared. The caisson had to be sufficiently buoyant, and also watertight, to enable the mortar to dry in the open air. It functioned as a kind of barge capable of supporting the block of mortar, for which purpose it had to be about two and a half to three times wider than the block of mortar (which had a density of approxima-tely 2.5 kg/m^3), since the draught of the caisson with its block would then be approximately equal to the height of the block to be set in place.

This explains the presence of planks and pieces of timber beneath the block, as well as that of vertical and obliquely angled timbers held fast in the mortar, which were used to make the caisson structurally rigid while it was being floated and lowered to the bottom. It also explains the absence of any vertical wooden walls, since these must have been removed after the block of mortar had been lowered to the bottom.

The double row of piles discovered at the eastern extremity of the island of Antirhodos is older (c. 400 BC) than the large blocks mentioned above. The presence of mortar at the lower end of the piles of the southern row indicates that these rows of piles must have been constructed in dry conditions, in other words that they were submerged after they were constructed.

We may postulate, therefore, that this double row of piles is the remnant of an ancient wooden quay. The piles of the sou-thern row have grooves into which planks were slotted to form a timber shuttering capable of holding a fill of quarry waste. The northern row had no such grooves, but could have supported wooden planking and have been sunk into the sea-bed to a depth of about 1m.

Oceanographic conditions in Alexandria

Winds

The following statistics (expressed in terms of percentage of time per directional sector) were provided by Alexandria's meteorologi-cal office for the period 1973–1992.

The first four lines of the table show the fre-quency of the wind in the four 90° sectors. The last two lines give the figures for the two 180° sectors: the N (E) S sector, or 'east wind' as we can call it, and the S (W) N sector, or 'west wind'. The last column gives the annual average. The following trends can be observed:

- on an annual average, the wind blows 2/3 of the time from the west and 1/3 of the time from the east;
- on an annual average, the winds blow from the W to N sector (NW) for a little more than half the time; these winds are therefore clearly prevailing;
- the summer winds (between June and September) blow from the NW sector for most of the time; only in October, then during the winter through May, do the winds blow from the east 35–40% of the time.

Winds

month	1	2	3	4	5	6	7	8	9	10	11	12	year
% of time per directional sector													
N to E	19	20	29	30	30	17	5	7	16	30	30	20	21
E to S	15	17	15	15	11	5	2	2	5	12	13	16	11
S to W	35	26	15	9	6	6	5	4	5	10	21	35	15
W to N	31	37	41	46	53	72	88	87	74	48	36	29	53
N (E) S	34	37	44	45	41	22	7	9	21	42	43	36	32
S (W) N	66	63	56	55	59	78	93	91	79	58	57	64	68

These figures demonstrate that sailing from Rome to Alexandria was a great deal easier than sailing in the opposite direction. The journey to Alexandria would have taken between two and three weeks, and the journey to Rome twice that time. Ships did on average two journeys a year, sailing during the summer season (May to September) in order to avoid the storms.

Waves

The following statistics have been obtained from observations carried out in the eastern Mediterranean aboard selected ships during the period 1960–1980.

The first four columns give the frequency of the swell in percentage of time for the sectors indicated. The fifth column gives the percentage of calm seas (and other sectors which do not reach Alexandria). The first line gives the periods of calm. The second line gives the periods of swell of less than 1m (height of the waves from crest to trough) and the third line the periods of swell of more than 1m. The following trends can be observed:

- off the coasts of Egypt and Libya the sea is calm for a little more than half the time;

- waves more than 1m high, which interfere with navigation by sail, occur for 25% of the time;
- waves from the W to N sector (approx. N285 to N5) represent 36% of the time and waves from the N to E sector (approx. N5 to N65) only represent 8% of the time.

Sea levels

The following levels have been recorded by the Egyptian authorities (in relation to the terrestrial datum point, Robert Zero):
LLWL (*lowest low water level*): -0.43m;
CD (chart datum or hydrographic zero): -0.34m;
MLWL (*mean low water level*): -0.05m;
MSL (*mean sea level*): 0.08m;
MHWL (*mean high water level*): 0.21m;
HHWL (*highest high water level*): 0.74m.
These figures show that the lowest water level is 9cm below the Hydro Zero and that mean sea level at Alexandria is 8cm above the Egyptian datum point.
It is worth mentioning that sea levels have changed during the last 2,500 years. Reduced to their simplest terms, scientific calculations show that sea levels have risen during this period by about 1.5m, or approximately 6cm per century. We might

add that the present trend indicates far higher increases: approximately 18cm for the last century (1880–1980) and, as currently estimated, 30–110cm for the 21st century.

Oscillations in mean sea levels appear to have occurred in the course of the last two millennia. It is very difficult, moreover, to distinguish eustatic movements (related to the sea) from tectonic movements (related to the earth). The example of Crete is illuminating, since over 2,000 years, the sea level has dropped between 4 and 8m in relation to the land at the western extremity of the island, whereas at its eastern end the sea level has risen between 1 and 4m during the same period.

It is currently accepted that at Alexandria the sea level has risen between 1 and 1.5m and that the land level has dropped between 5 and 6m over the last 2,000 years.

It is also worth noting that tsunamis have been reported on the coasts of the Middle East.

Sedimentology

The sediments found on the beaches and the sea-bed adjoining the roads at Alexandria are made up of sands whose granulometry (D50) ranges between 0.20 and 0.50mm. These sands almost certainly come from ancient deposits of the Nile. The beaches at Alexandria have been experiencing generalised erosion for some decades now and a number of conservation measures (re-sanding of the beaches, creation of rough stone embankments) have been taken with varying degrees of success. The erosion is principally due to the displacement of sand from the beach towards the open sea which occurs during storms.

In addition to this movement of sand out to sea, significant displacement also occurs along the coast, both from east to west and west to east. Experts calculate that these opposing movements are each in the order of 100,000m³ a year, and therefore cancel one another out. It is obvious from this that if an obstacle were constructed at right angles to the coast, 100,000m³ of sand a year would be deposited on either side of the obstacle. This is what must have happened after the construction of the Heptastadion, at least a proportion of these deposits coming to rest against its sides each year.

Waves

sector	N285-N325	N325-N5	N5-N35	N35-N65	calms	total
H<0.1m	-	-	-	-	56	56
0.1>H>1m	10	6	2	2	-	20
H>1m	13	7	2	2	-	24
total	23	13	4	4	56	100

The *navalia*

There were powerful reasons why archaeologists should be interested in the eastern half of the Portus Magnus: the ancient coastline was still discernible here beneath the sea, and adjoining it were the royal quarters. The western half of the harbour, less often mentioned in the ancient texts, was excavated at a later date. On the site of the current fishing port, its coastline is largely obscured by the construction of the modern corniche road, so this part of the bay was unlikely to surrender its secrets easily.

The submerged remains of a large quay. Although we fully expected to find architectural remains in the royal quarters, we had no reason to anticipate such impressive structures on the western side of the Portus Magnus.

The ancient coastline could be traced from Cape Lochias as far as the section of coast that faces the island of Antirhodos. We continued our survey of the bay by proceeding westwards from this point. Our first surprise came at the midpoint of the corniche – which yielded absolutely nothing. The current shoreline was actually underwater in Ptolemaic times and because it is now so extensively built up it is impossible to form an impression of the original coastline (although it was probably set very much further back). There were no remains to be found here, therefore. Further along, however, in the south-west of the bay, we came across some huge submerged forms. After producing relief maps of the sea-bed and examining the loose sediment in order to determine the contours of any solid structures, we decided to proceed from a visible point and demarcate the submerged mass by working our way along its edge. Little by little, as our team of divers drew off the sediment, the outlines of a vast harbour structure emerged, fitted out with numerous quays. We drew up a new map, showing the current contours of the structure, from which we were able to reconstruct the ancient contours as we may suppose them to have been prior to the occurrence of subsidence, rock falls and natural accretions due to the deposition of sediments by marine currents.

The structure facing the Heptastadion resembled a peninsula connected to the island of Pharos and extended at several points by long quays and breakwaters expertly constructed from blocks of limestone. It was protected by a natural island situated to the north and partly paved, and itself formed a bulwark for the Heptastadion, sheltering it from the full onslaught of the sea. The harbour quays are paved in limestone, and ancient mortar foundations, paving stones, limestone construction blocks and fragments of red granite columns attest the presence of a small monument situated on the central mole.

Much further north, near the fort of Qait-Bey, an impressive harbour installation composed of a number of docks has been discovered. The collapsed platforms tell us something about the construction technique (see the chapter on Antirhodos) using piles set in a buttress of loose rocks, sheeting piles, enormous mortar blocks and areas of paving. The size of the quays and the remains of walls suggest that large buildings may once have stood on this site. The whole configuration dates from the Roman period, when Alexandria's harbour structures appear to have undergone a general programme of alterations: the piles of the

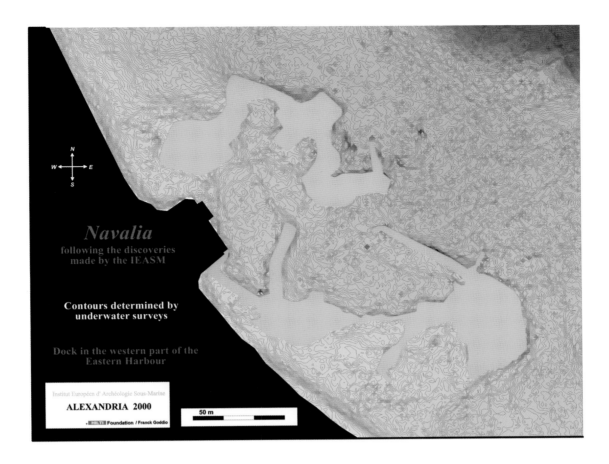

Navalia
following the discoveries
made by the IEASM

**Contours determined by
underwater surveys**

Dock in the western part of the
Eastern Harbour

Institut Européen d' Archéologie Sous-Marine

ALEXANDRIA 2000

Foundation / Franck Goddio

50 m

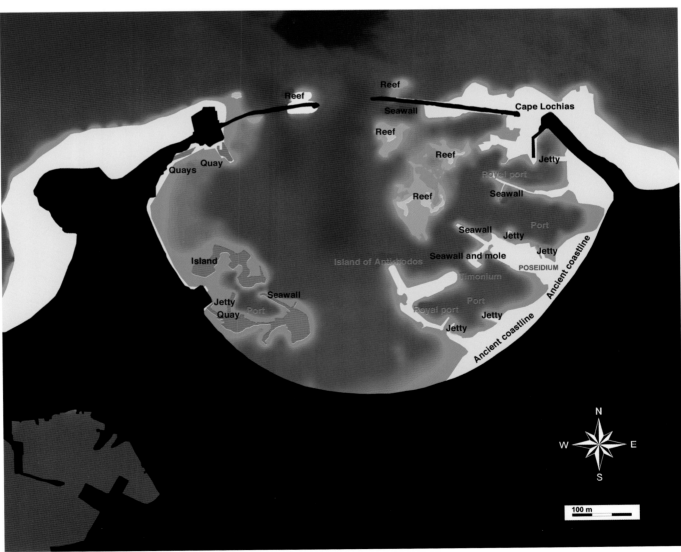

*Map of the Portus Magnus
with the western navalia
shown in red.*

Wooden piles used to reinforce the foundations of structures built along the shores of the island of Pharos. Among the piles of small limestone blocks which they held in place, architectural fragments of ancient monuments were discovered.

northern mole, for example, are identical to those that form the subfoundations of the Poseidium. Was this part of a major renovation programme? And if so why at this time?

The discovery of this site particularly impressed us: everything was bigger and more beautiful than we had imagined from the texts. We were walking underwater on magnificent causeways that were still in excellent condition, endeavouring to imagine what they must have looked like when they were actually in use and stood a good two metres above the water level. By establishing the precise topography of the area we have been able to confirm that this part of the island of Pharos has sunk by 7m since the 2nd century, a fact that gave us our first clue as to the location of the famous lighthouse.

The shipyards

The area that we were studying was the site of the ancient shipyards.

Now there is an island in the surging sea in front of Egypt,

and men call it Pharos,

distant as far as a hollow ship runs in a whole day

when the shrill wind blows fair behind her.

Therein is a harbour with good anchorage,

whence men launch the shapely ships into the sea,

when they have drawn supplies of black water [i.e., water in deep places, where the light cannot reach it].

There for twenty days the gods kept me,

nor ever did the winds that blow over the deep spring up,

which speed men's ships over the broad back of the sea.

So speaks Ulysses, hero of Homer's *Odyssey* (IV, 355, trans. A.T. Murray, Heinemann, 1966): the island of Pharos was clearly one of the many places where he stopped with his crew. Indeed, Pharos is one of the only islands off the coast of Egypt. A thousand years later, Alexander the Great was quick to recognise the geographical advantages of the site with its potential double harbour. The Ptolemies constructed a large mole linking Pharos to the mainland, since which time the area has been extended so much with rock fills and sedimentary deposits that it is easy to forget that Pharos was originally an island.

Opposite and above: paving found on the moles of the navalia and the Pharos docks. The tops of wooden piles can be seen between the paving stones.

**Sheet-pile walls on the site
of the Pharos moles.**

This whole section of the coast was given over to the shipyards, or *navalia*, where Alexandrian ships were constructed and others overhauled. Alexandria was one of the most important centres for naval construction in Egypt, despite the fact that the country was short of wood, the only varieties to be found there being tamarisk, acanthus and palm, none of them suitable for construction purposes. The pharaohs of the Old and New Kingdoms imported wood from as far afield as Lebanon and Somaliland. The Ptolemies acquired their supplies in Phoenicia, Cyprus or Asia Minor, constructing both their commercial and their naval vessels from long conifer trunks, which had the advantage of combining flexibility with strength. The siege of the city by Caesar, as described by Caesar himself, demonstrates the vigour of Alexandria's shipbuilding industry. *Although the Alexandrians had lost more than a hundred and ten long vessels in the harbour and the shipyards, they were determined to reassemble their fleet, he tells us. [...] On every branch of the Nile, patrol boats were stationed for the purpose of collecting tolls. Lying neglected in the palace dockyards were old boats that had not seen service for many a long year; these were repaired, and others were brought back to Alexandria. Porticoes, gymnasia and public buildings were dismantled, and the planks thus obtained fulfilled the function of oars, where these items were missing. Native ingenuity supplied one thing, the city's*

An excavated area of the navalia.

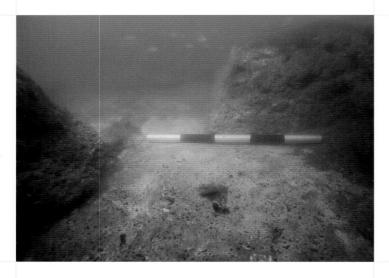

Moles in the navalia.

We knew that the shores of Pharos were the site of the ancient shipyards, but the remains we uncovered suggested that the scale of these harbour installations greatly exceeded anything we might have imagined.

resources another. […] And so, in the space of a few days, against all expectations, twenty-two quadriremes and five quinqueremes were completed, with the addition of a goodly number of smaller, open boats. The shipyards must have been well equipped indeed and the builders enormously skilled to have accomplished so much.

We also know of two other, truly exceptional ships that were built at Alexandria. The first, as described by Athenaeus, whose description is reported by Callixeinus of Rhodes, was 129m long. Built at the behest of Ptolemy IV Philopator, it had 40 banks of oars, two stem-posts armed with seven rams, two stern-posts and four rudders. A special shipyard had to be built for the construction of this one ship, which required as much wood as would have been used to build 50 quinqueremes, and a canal had to be dug on site in order to launch it.

Ptolemy Philopator's royal ship was an even more extravagant affair. Built of rare woods such as thuya, cedar, Milesian cypress and tropical varieties, it was a floating palace, divided into numerous rooms (hence its name: 'Thalamega'), banqueting halls, porticoes and galleries, all decorated with ivory, gilded bronze and costly hangings.

The poets from whom we learn these details have no doubt embellished their subject, but they give us an idea, nevertheless, of the scale of shipbuilding activities at Alexandria: like the city itself, the industry it fostered was gigantic.

A hive of commerce

We may suppose that the harbour sheltered by the island in this western corner of the Portus Magnus was a place of transit for ships bound for the Eunostos and preparing to make their way across the Heptastadion. This long mole, built at the time of the Ptolemies, was intersected by two channels. It was thus possible to reach Alexandria from any of its harbours regardless of the weather, and the city depended on this ease of access: it was to become the 'counting house of the world', in other words a centre for maritime trade with the entire Mediterranean basin. It is probable therefore that these shores we were surveying once housed vast repositories, called 'treasures' in the Greek of the papyri. These public granaries operated in a similar way to banks. Officials known as *sitologos* managed the stocks of corn as if it were money, taking receipt of goods deposited by individuals and making payments to them, in return for which they themselves were remunerated. Alexandria was regarded in a wider sense as Rome's granary, since a large part of Egypt's cereal production was exported by way of Alexandria. The Roman emperors were perfectly aware of this dependence and prohibited their senators from entering Egypt, since confiscating Alexandria's corn would have been tantamount to starving Rome.

Goods upon which the economy not only of Egypt but also of a large part of the Mediterranean depended were conveyed, therefore, via Alexandria. The Alexandrian miracle is that such an activity could have flourished on a site so geographically ill adapted to it.

Large pink granite column base forming part of a protective barrier built of blocks and architectural elements taken from demolished monuments. Shoreline of the navalia.

Fragment of a cornice used as filling material, found among the loose rubble of the moles in the navalia.

The lighthouse

*One of the Seven Wonders of the Ancient World, the Lighthouse of Alexandria
was so famous that its name, 'Pharos', became the generic word for lighthouse in Latin.*

**The lighthouse at Alexandria represented on
a coin dating from the reign of Antoninus
Pius, 140 AD.**
© The British Museum

The lighthouse at Alexandria was not the only, or even the first, structure of its kind; but it was colossal, towering probably some 100m above the sea. The Greeks were familiar with the idea of light signals and adopted a system of lighting fires on hilltops bordering the shore. The rugged Greek coastline made such a system feasible, but there were no such clifftops at Alexandria: the lighthouse had to be built well offshore, and it had to be tall if it was to warn ships of the many reefs bordering the fairway which gave access to the bay. The oldest document relating to the lighthouse is an epigram attributed to Posidippus, a poet living at the court of Ptolemy II Philadelphus (284–246 BC), who financed the building's construction: *Lord Proteus: the saviour of Hellenes, this watchman of Pharos, was built by Sostratus, son of Dexiphanes, a Cnidian. In Egypt there are no mountain-peaks, as in the islands: but low lies the breakwater where ships may harbour. Therefore this tower, cleaving the sky straight and upright, shines in the daytime countless leagues away: and all night long the sailor who runs with the waves shall see a great light blazing from the summit. And he may run even to the Bull's Horn, and yet not miss the God of Safety, O Proteus, whosoever sails this way.*

Sostratus' clever ploy

There may be other mysteries relating to the lighthouse, but we do know that it was built by Sostratus of Cnidus, a first-rate architect and engineer – and something of a trickster. According to the satirical poet Lucian of Samosata (c. 120–180 AD) – whose story is worth repeating, even if we cannot actually verify it – Sostratus engraved his own name on the stone, then plastered it over and added the name of the royal couple of the time. Once the plaster had worn away, as it was bound to over time, all that would be retained for posterity was the following inscription: *Sostratus of Cnidus, son of Dexiphanes, [dedicates this building] to the gods who protect us, for the safety of sailors.*

The work began circa 290 BC and the monument was inaugurated some 10 years later.

What did it look like?

Caesar alludes to *a very tall tower of marvellous construction, built on an island whose name it bears,* and Strabo describes the tower as *having several storeys, in white marble, a work of wondrous beauty.* Flavius Josephus specifies that *its light travels 300 stadia* (approximately 50km). Alexandrian coins, minted between the reign of Domitian (81–96 AD) and that of Commodus (180–192 AD), provide the best iconographic source, showing the lighthouse as a three-storied tower, wider at the base than at the summit, with two vertical rows of apertures let into its walls. A door with a flight of steps leading up to it is clearly indicated as the means of access, and the first storey is decorated with Tritons sounding trumpets, while a statue (Poseidon or Ptolemy in divine guise) appears at the summit of the tower.

Two late mosaics, an engraved glass found at Begram, in Afghanistan (probably a souvenir brought back from Alexandria), and three terracotta lamps in the shape of a lighthouse provide additional details, from which we may gather that the first storey was square, the second octagonal and the third cylindrical, an arrangement which appears to have influenced the construction of numerous Arabic minarets.

__Coin dating from the reign of Commodus, showing the Lighthouse of Alexandria.__
*© **The British Museum***

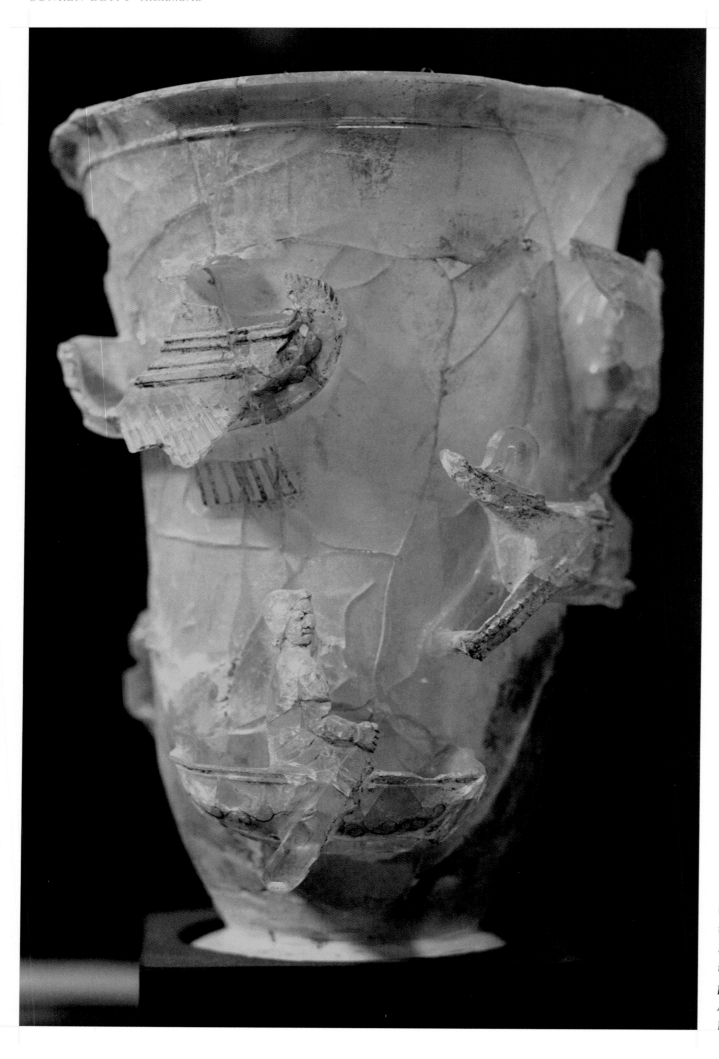

This page and opposite: the two sides of the Begram vase, in Afghanistan.
Photos © John C. Huntington, images reproduced with the permission of The Huntington Archive of Buddhist and Related Arts

Flights of fancy

Arab chroniclers subsequently provided some 30 descriptions of the lighthouse, but their enthusiasm for their subject led them to invent certain details that were technically implausible. Some speak of a mirror of polished steel that reflected the image of ships before they even appeared on the horizon, whereas it is more likely in fact that a large fire burned at the summit. It is possible that the fuel for the fire – faggots perhaps, or torches of particularly resinous wood, or mineral oils burned in large basins – was hoisted up to the third storey using special lifting equipment. In addition, an optical device of some kind (corresponding to the mirror referred to in the texts) may have diffused the light from the fire to produce an intermittent signal.

Other authors describe a group of metal statues, one of which was manipulated by a complicated mechanism so that it moved along its axis, following the course of the sun in the sky. While it is true that Alexandrian engineers had a reputation for being able to create moving figures, and that the statues of Tritons and of Poseidon were probably made of bronze, more than that we cannot say.

Finally, Arab authors claim that the foundations of the building were composed of vaults and arches made of glass, and rested underground on four pieces of metal called 'crabs'. There is an analogy here with the four bronze crabs which supported the Alexandrian obelisk conserved in New York. What is more, glass manufacture was a particularly flourishing industry in Alexandria, and glassware was a major export product – and yet how are we seriously to imagine a lighthouse made of glass?

What we do know is that the lighthouse had several rooms, which housed those responsible for guarding the building and looking after the equipment. We can readily imagine that a great many people would have been required to man such a structure.

When a myth crumbles

We have very little information regarding the state of the monument in antiquity. Ammianus Marcellinus tells us that the lighthouse was built for Cleopatra (69–30 BC), and although we know that this was not the case, it is possible that the building was restored on her orders. According to Procopius of Gaza, the Byzantine emperor Anastasius I, who reigned from 491 to 518 AD, had the foundations repaired after they were damaged by the sea: *A tower that brings succour to those sailors who have wandered off course by lighting the saving fire of Poseidon, it is this that I follow; I was on the point of pitching beneath the blast and din of the winds, when I was restored by the attentions of Ammonios, 'father of the emperor'*, recounts an epigram from the *Palatine Anthology*.

In 950 AD, an earthquake cracked the building, and six years later the fire chamber collapsed. Further damage was recorded in 1261, then again (particularly serious this time) in 1303. A Montpellier cartulary even gives the exact date of the building's destruction as 8 August 1303, although the texts contradict one another in this regard. According to a description by Ibn Battuta, in April 1326, only one façade was destroyed, but in 1349 the same author writes: *Having gone to the lighthouse on my return from the Maghreb [Morocco, Algeria and Tunisia], in the year 750 [of the Hegira], I discovered it in such a ruinous state that it was no longer possible to enter, or to reach the door which granted access to it.*

The lighthouse listed in the 3rd century by Philo of Byzantium as one of the Seven Wonders of the World was the most recent of these ancient marvels, and yet this structure must have stood for more than 15 centuries, surviving the onslaught of winds and tides and the natural catastrophes that wrought havoc with the rest of the city.

What can we say about this lighthouse, which was so famous that people continued to describe it even after it had disappeared? Are we really talking about the same building? Is it not more likely that it was rebuilt, maybe several times, and not necessarily on the same spot? There are numerous hypotheses and no certainties.

So where was it?

Writing at the end of the 15th century, the chronicler Ibn Iyas records that in 1477–9 the Sultan Qait-Bey built the fortress that is still standing today on the site of the ancient lighthouse. Logically enough, therefore, almost every cartographer since the 18th century has situated the lighthouse on the site of the Qait-Bey fort. The fort certainly reused some earlier architectural elements, but these date from Roman times and could not therefore have formed part of the lighthouse, as was once assumed. A jumble of architectural blocks lie submerged at the base of the fort, and again it was presumed that these might be the remains of the lighthouse. And yet is that logically possible? Could these sections of pink and grey granite have been window mouldings, when Strabo tells us, and two Arab chroniclers confirm, that the lighthouse was in fact built of white stone? And had it stood on this site, where would it have been directing ships, if not towards the dangerous eastern reefs? In 1892, Wilhelm Sieglin proposed a different location, some 500m east of the fort, on the largest of the reefs, marking one of the extremities of the main fairway. In order to test these various hypotheses we needed to refer to our precise geophysical survey of the region.

Ship entering the harbour at Alexandria, engraving on a 3rd-century sarcophagus. © *The art archive*

171

The topographical evidence

There are numerous different ways of interpreting the ancient texts, and archaeological excavations had not as yet permitted us to draw firm conclusions concerning the provenance of the submerged rubble lying at the base of the fort, outside the harbour. This debris is so extensive (see 13 on the map on p. 49), and such an oddly assorted jumble, that it appears to derive from a number of different buildings, dating from different times, haphazardly thrown down to serve as a protective barrier, or to block a channel leading into the harbour. Our only recourse, therefore, was to rely on the topographical evidence.

Having surveyed the whole of the Portus Magnus, we now knew that the difference in ground level past and present, due to the combined factors of subsidence and rising water, exceeded 7m. The top of the Pharos moles, dating from the 2nd century, was now 5.5m below the water level, and given tidal variations in the Mediterranean and the protective function of the moles, the latter must originally have projected a good 2m above the average water level. It was important to keep this difference in mind as we considered the facts. Applying what we know about the topography of the region, we can see that the present-day site of the Qait-Bey fort must originally have been a raised promontory on the shoreward side of the island of Pharos. The reefs lying to the western side of the fort today, on a level with the shore, were then 6m above sea level. How then could the lighthouse, if it was situated at this point, have been surrounded by water, as Strabo tells us? *The point itself of the island [Pharos] is a rock battered from all sides by the waves and bearing a tower of white stone, admirably constructed, having several levels, whose name is the same as the island's,* he writes. And, more importantly, from such a position would it not have sent ships hurtling towards the reefs that lay between the two harbour channels? For we need to picture them also standing 7m higher than at present.

Whatever the actual position of the lighthouse, some sort of structure was certainly necessary at this spot to signal to navigators the dangers posed by the reefs that had emerged between the two fairways (see 12 on the map on p. 49), and the remains of a structure have in fact been discovered here. These large limestone blocks, 1.7m in length, extending, on the harbour side, below the concrete breakwater constructed in 1917, are probably a small part of the structural remains located beneath the water by the engineer of Alexandria's harbours, M. Jondet, before the construction of the breakwater obscured this precious evidence. It is tempting to imagine that these blocks may originally have constituted the subfoundations of a large monument, perhaps the lighthouse itself. Thus located, surrounded by water on all sides, it would have occupied a strategic position, capable of defending the two harbour channels against the intrusions of enemy fleets, as mentioned in the texts.

The geophysical surveys would seem to support this hypothesis, but perhaps future research will shed new light on what remains an intriguing mystery.

The shape of the Taposiris Magna tower matches some descriptions of the Lighthouse of Alexandria.
© Photo Soheir Bakhoum

Conclusion

In 1992, Egypt's Supreme Council for Antiquities approved a proposal by the European Institute of Underwater Archaeology (IEASM) to carry out research in the harbour at Alexandria. The objective was clear: to establish the topography of the submerged regions and substructures, and to draw up a map corresponding as closely as possible to the region as it appeared in antiquity. The following procedures were adopted: data collection and analysis, topographical surveying, diving expeditions in precisely selected areas, excavations to determine the characteristics of the sites, examination of the artefacts and publication of conclusions and plausible hypotheses. The measures taken differed little from those adopted for the study of junks and Western vessels like the *San Diego*, discovered in the China Sea.

The difference lay in the scale of an operation whose object was not a wreck, but the submerged sections of an entire metropolis. The Alexandrian remains were extensive, difficult to handle and scattered over a large area, so that methods for recording data and gathering epigraphic information had to be found whereby objects could be left *in situ*. Working conditions were also very different from those that prevailed in the depths of the China Sea on account of heavy natural sedimentation and the polluting effects of urban waste. We may have been diving in shallow water (averaging a depth of 5m and reaching a maximum of 15m) – in contrast to operations conducted off the Philippines – but our research involved a formidable dive back in time.

Starting afresh with the maps

The existing maps were not the archaeological maps they purported to be, tending more often than not to be historical. Although they gave the impression of reflecting information that had been independently acquired, in fact they simply reproduced the interpretation given by Mahmoud Bey El-Falaky in 1866. For many years, cartographers dedicated to producing a map of Alexandria gave free reign to their imaginations, using a history of events as the basis for their conclusions. They dreamed of finding Alexander's tomb, or Cleopatra's, or the library, or the remains of the lighthouse itself. This romantic perspective was fuelled by the expectations of a certain public, in which the individual cults of great men, great works and great archaeologists, were ultimately encompassed in a single passion.

Such an approach is legitimate. As the capital of the Graeco-Macedonian Pharaohs and a showcase of Hellenistic culture, Alexandria has assumed a quasi-mythical status, inviting generations of historians and archaeologists to dream about its glorious past. It was this in part that attracted the IEASM to its shores; but we had to confine our reveries to the nights spent on board the *Princess Duda*, if we wished to adopt an effective, scientific approach during the day. After surveying the area visually and taking magnetometric readings, we decided to begin with the more accessible, eastern half of the Portus Magnus, where the submerged sections of the Ptolemaic royal quarters or *basileia* were commonly located, reserving the western part for a later date.

Following extensive surveys and diving expeditions, we were able to confirm that we had located and mapped the submerged monuments and harbours dating from the time of the Ptolemies – and that all we had uncovered of this city of dreams was a collection of enigmatic fragments.

The intense pleasure associated with each new discovery was prolonged by the excitement of searching for clues which might help to provide the answers to our questions. What did the sculptures and the inscriptions we found represent in their own time? How, when and by what processes were they reduced to such a pitiful state? Was it the result of a natural disaster or of actions undertaken by the authorities during Ptolemaic times?

The smooth running of our operations depended upon the collaboration of a great many specialists – epigraphers, archaeologists, engineers, geophysicists, ceramics experts and numismatists – who could discuss the problems of interpretation raised by our discoveries and help to refine our methods of investigation. As a result of these combined efforts we learnt that the topography of this crucial area of Alexandria – the harbours serving the *basileia* – was radically different from what had originally been assumed. The actual harbour layout makes better sense technically than the assumed layout, facilitating safe access into the harbour basins by minimising the impact of waves and swell. The long causeway which appeared on the early maps as the site of the Timonium did not actually exist, and what was depicted as an area of shallow water with the island of Antirhodos emerging out of it is in fact the peninsula. The island itself has a different shape from the one that it was previously given and does in fact shelter a magnificent little harbour, as the texts suggest. In terms of both position and layout, the 'private royal harbour' mentioned by Strabo is both more functional and more aesthetically pleasing than in its original reconstruction.

Several channels of inquiry

The conclusions we have drawn concerning the topography of the Portus Magnus may be regarded as definitive: our map is based directly on quantifiable realities and confirms the ancient texts. Using it as a starting point, we have been able to ask engineering questions regarding the choice of site and the architecture of the ancient harbour. Having identified the specific sites of Ptolemaic palaces and temples mentioned by Strabo, we cannot claim, however, to have found the monuments themselves. What we have uncovered to date are vast areas, partially paved and strewn with debris, which, thanks to their immersion, have escaped the fate of those exposed parts of the city that were either built over or destroyed. We are in no position to provide immediate dates for the construction of buildings here or the events that reduced them to this expanse of jumbled ruins.

One important point has been established: the ground is still covered with limestone paving which for the most part has retained its continuity and coherence. On top of this paving lie blocks, some of them contiguous, testifying to the existence of ancient walls, as well as column fragments, lintels and other architectural vestiges constructed of limestone, marble, pink granite or quartzite. Here and there, we find monoliths from pre-Alexandrian Pharaonic temples which have been reused in the fabric of the walls. In among the piles of stone, it has also been possible to identify a few structures still in place such as solidly built walls of bonded limestone and, in rare instances, remnants of walls constructed from baked clay.

Our ancient coastline corresponds to surveys made in the 19th century, based on the study of contours still visible beneath the sea.

Since antiquity, the monuments built in Alexandria under the Ptolemies and the Caesars are known to have suffered violent disturbances, the direct or indirect consequences of tectonic phenomena which have periodically rocked or toppled them, but also the result of human intervention. We can confirm that a great many architectural elements have been reused since antiquity. On excavated sites, there are manifest gaps in the remains that have been uncovered, the absence of certain elements illustrating the multiple extractions that have occurred over the course of time, leading to the recycling of columns, capitals, lintels and statues in the construction of new monuments.

As regards the history of the Portus Magnus, there is still little available evidence upon which to base a chronology of significant events. The presence of broken statues leads us to suspect that the iconoclastic fervour which marked the introduction of Christianity in the 4th century also took its toll here. Buildings which had collapsed probably served as quarry materials, as the instances of dispersion suggest and the remains of stone-sawing workshops confirm.

The harbour installations at Alexandria appear to date from the Ptolemaic era, but the numerous columns of smooth granite and the baked clay walls are Roman and Byzantine. The monument excavated at the base of the peninsula is probably the remains of a temple, and the ruins along the coast may be the remains of the royal palaces, but we cannot say with any certainty: the layout of the area is likely to have been affected by the major urban renovation programmes and buildings constructed during the Hellenistic dynasty have almost certainly disappeared.

Part of the international team researching the Portus Magnus.

What we can say is that the palace occupied by Cleopatra on the island of Antirhodos (dating from well before her reign) was located opposite the Timonium built by Mark Antony. To the extent that their palaces retain an air of ghostly unreality, the phantoms of those two lovers continue to exercise a powerful effect on our imagination. The ground, however, gives us some clues as to what became of these royal dwellings.

A number of hypotheses

Radiocarbon dating has shown that the jetty on the eastern point of the island dates from the 5th and 4th centuries BC, which may seem surprising to the historian who clings to the image of Alexander founding his city on a virgin site. Although earlier dynasties exercised the same rigorous police and customs controls vis-à-vis Greek navigators and merchants as the Saitic and Persian kings, we also know that the Pharaohs employed the services of mercenaries, whom they brought over from Greece. These hired men could not have been treated like suspected pirates or contrabandists. Perhaps the shelter offered by the little bay on the shoreward side of Pharos, where they would have put into port, was the site of structures built to accommodate them.

The paving of the esplanade, on the island of Antirhodos, was apparently constructed under the first Ptolemies, since radiocarbon dating shows that the wooden formwork dates from the 3rd century BC. The seven plinths bearing Greek inscriptions extolling the Emperor Caracalla are evidence of an occupation of the site in the 3rd century AD (c. 213). We may ask whether the palace occupied by Cleopatra, three centuries earlier, still existed at that time, but there is no way of knowing.

As for the sculptures (the two sphinxes and the priest), they were probably the remains of a sanctuary dedicated to Isis. At the moment of their fall, the sculptures smashed certain items of pottery, and these shards furnish precious evidence regarding dates. The sculptures themselves evidently escaped the depredations of Christian iconoclasts, who set about destroying pagan idols during the period leading up to 360 AD and intermittently until the end of the 5th century. We can explain this by the fact that the ground where they lay was already submerged at this date – and so we can situate the earthquake which caused the shores to collapse within a specific time bracket. The existence of some 50 columns shattered by their fall, all lying in the same direction, corroborates this hypothesis regarding a violent disturbance.

The shores at Alexandria appear therefore to have suffered both sudden and formidable catastrophes (earthquakes accompanied by tidal waves) and the gradual phenomena of subsidence and rising sea levels, which completed the process of destruction by engulfing the fallen monuments.

As our theories developed, we compared our interpretations with the literary sources. In doing so, it was important to distinguish between those authors who, like Strabo, were genuine eyewitnesses and those who compiled second-hand information and added their own embellishments.

Exceptional pieces of statuary

Our excavations were rewarded by the discovery of a number of extraordinary objects. Three fragments, of an obelisk, a plinth and a statue, dating from the Rameside era and eight sections of a building constructed by the Saitic king Apries (589–570 BC) were re-used in monuments dating from dynasties prior to the arrival of Alexander. They confirm that the majority of works of Pharaonic antiquity that have been found in Graeco-Roman Alexandria originated in the temples of

Heliopolis. The statuary remains are remarkable. There is a moving beauty about the marble head (thought to represent the features of a Roman empress), plunged in the murky depths of the sea, and the torso of the god Hermes is a magnificent testament to the talent of Hellenistic sculptors. Preserved almost intact, the figure of a priest clasping a Canopic vase containing the relics of Osiris seems to express an almost tender piety towards the saviour-god who gives new life to the initiates of Isis. In the vast *basileia* situated on the sea front, a royal colossus and two classical sphinxes were discovered. These works in a Pharaonic style, carved from granite in the Graeco-Roman era, would have stood before the façade of royal or religious buildings advertising the divine power of the sovereign. In the same area, there is a gigantic head of a monumental sphinx with a raptor's face, an image embodying in all probability a universal protector god, concocted by the priesthood and invoked by the sorcerers of Roman Egypt. Further on, two animal statues, a granite serpent in the Hellenistic style and a typically Egyptian limestone ibis (probably both close to their original location) represent two gods who were particularly venerated by the Alexandrians: the guardian spirit upon whom depended the fate of the city and its inhabitants, and the god of wisdom and knowledge, Thoth, otherwise known as Hermes Trismegistus ('the-thrice-greatest').

These finds should clearly be viewed in tandem with other divine effigies which were recorded in the adjacent areas, today built over by the corniche: a small statue of Harpocrates and statues of Isis and the lioness-headed Sekhmet. We cannot assume, however, that this region contained as many temples as there are gods represented there: the patron of every important temple, whether Egyptian or Greek, tolerated the worship of other gods and the display of their images. This sometimes led to a secondary cult dedicated to these 'resident' gods, some of whom were offered to the common people as a special object of worship. We can readily imagine that the falcon-headed sphinx with his kindly ears, the guardian of the city, and the god Thoth-Hermes had a space allotted to them in the open parts of the temple or in temple annexes.

After more than 10,000 dives and 10 years of research, we were at last in a position to produce a precise topographical map of the submerged areas of ancient Alexandria. And even if there are still as many unanswered questions as there are recovered artefacts, at least future archaeologists will be able to proceed from a solid base. Our approach was, of necessity, scientific and laborious, and yet the mythical glow that bathes this ancient city remains undimmed, despite the incursions of reality; if these gave the dream clearer outlines, they did nothing to diminish the fascination which the city exercises today on anyone curious about the past.

Postscript

The first dive at a site is always an unforgettable moment – a preliminary inspection of unknown remains which have been lying for centuries, absorbed and modified by life on the ocean bed. Nature has reclaimed its rights and transformed these works of man into bizarre sculptures composed of corals, sponges and limestone, which completely envelop the objects, turning them into living works of art. What secrets, one wonders, are waiting to be discovered beneath this dense mantle?

There is a thrill in drifting gently towards these relics, just brushing them with one's hand, swimming up a little higher and looking again, floating over the scene, like one of the fish which have made this place their home. It is a moment of pure privilege when you find yourself gazing at this mysterious spectacle, admiring it, and knowing that you are the first to do so. Each time I have the – quite unreasonable – feeling that this unique tableau, never seen by a human being before, came together, as if by magic, at the very moment that I set eyes on it. This impression accords strangely with the French expression 'inventer un site' (to discover a site).

The discovery of what remains of the royal quarters submerged in the harbour at Alexandria, with all its dramatic encounters, was even more exciting, infinitely so in fact, than coming face to face with an unexplored wreck.

After its shipwreck, a vessel carries on travelling; not in space, but in time. Concealed from human sight, it continues its secret and solitary journey, for centuries to come, and its discovery and excavation ought not to signal the end of this long odyssey.

When I excavate a wreck, I feel as if I am cutting a mysterious tie which has held this ship fast, for centuries, at the bottom of the ocean. Free of its moorings once more, it can sail on towards new adventures – those of knowledge and learning – and new countries, beyond the far horizon.

When the cargo of a ship which, centuries earlier, failed to put safely into port now arrives in a modern-day harbour, the impression created is a strange one. It seems as if history has resumed its course, and a tragic interlude has been closed off in parentheses. Here too, on the site of Alexandria's Portus Magnus, history deposited its cargo of mysterious monuments and relics, and this cargo has been hauled into our own times, where we are unravelling its secrets, little by little.

Anyone who discovers a site has a responsibility as regards the new life of this forgotten inheritance which he has brought back into the light of day. One of the great pleasures that archaeology affords is the organisation of international exhibitions following the restoration and study of recovered artefacts. The interest shown by the public (of all ages) in these exhibited artefacts legitimises the archaeologist's search for and retrieval of ancient objects. For those who took part, it represents a deeply rewarding conclusion to any archaeological mission.

The underwater excavations of ancient Alexandria have enabled us to draw a precise map of the Portus Magnus. They have also brought to light archaeological treasures which furnish us with valuable information regarding the history of the city. These treasures are a testimony, in some cases of exceptional beauty, to the greatness of one of the most amazing cities of antiquity.

Franck Goddio, Director of the IEASM

Glossary

Aboukir town situated 35km north-east of Alexandria. On 1 August 1798, Nelson defeated the French fleet in Aboukir Bay.

Achilles Tatius 3rd-century writer who celebrated the splendour of Alexandria in his fictional *Leucippe and Clitophon*, written in Greek.

Actium promontory at the entrance to the Gulf of Ambracia (present-day Arta), where Octavian and Agrippa defeated the naval forces of Mark Antony in 31 BC.

aegyptiaca term commonly used to designate the recording and studying of Egyptian finds made outside Egypt and the Sudan.

Aeschylus (525–456 BC), Greek dramatist, author of more than 80 tragedies, only seven of which are still in existence.

Agathocles tutor, together with Sosibios, of the young Ptolemy V.

Agathodaimon Egyptian serpent god, the 'good spirit' responsible for bringing the waters of the Nile to Alexandria.

Agrippa *Agrippa Marcus Vipsanius* (63–12 BC), Roman general, chief adviser and later son-in-law of Augustus, who organised a sort of co-regency for him. He commanded at Actium.

Alcibiades (450–404 BC), Athenian general responsible for the Athenian disaster during the Sicilian campaign. Pupil and lover of Socrates.

Alexander the Great (356–323 BC), son of Philip II of Macedonia and Olympias. He founded the city of Alexandria in 331 BC.

Ambracia situated on the lower course of the Arachthus. Present-day Arta in western Greece.

Ammianus Marcellinus (c. 340–400 AD), Roman writer who refers to the foundation of Alexandria in his *History*.

Amon Theban god known, under the name of Amon-Ra, as the 'king of the gods' and the patron of the conquerors of the New Empire, who dedicated the largest temple in Egypt to him, at Karnak. Represented in human form, though sometimes with a ram's head.

Amset Egyptian god, son of Horus, represented with a human head.

Anastasius I Byzantine emperor who reigned from 491–518 AD.

Antirhodos island in Alexandria's eastern harbour.

Antonia Minor daughter of Mark Antony and Octavia, born in 37 BC, future mother of Germanicus and Claudius.

Antony *Marcus Antonius* (83–30 BC), Roman general who married Cleopatra VII.

Anubis patron god of embalmers. Represented as a wild dog or a jackal. He was responsible for conducting the dead to the other world.

Api Egyptian god, son of Horus, represented with a baboon's head.

Apis Egyptian god, represented in the form of a bull. He had a sanctuary at Memphis.

Apollodorus of Athens mythographer of the 1st or 2nd century AD. There were a number of poets by the same name, which was very popular and signifies 'gift of Apollo'.

Appian (2nd century AD), author of *Rome's Civil Wars*, in Greek. He mentions Caesar's arrival at Alexandria.

Aristophanes (445–385 BC), famous Greek comic dramatist, from Athens.

Aristotle (384–322 BC), Greek philosopher and scholar of immense learning. He was a pupil of Plato and tutor to Alexander the Great.

Arrian (c. 105–180 AD), author of the *History of Alexander: The Anabasis of Alexander the Great*, written in Greek, on the basis of early testimonies.

Artemision (Cape) promontory on the northern side of the island of Euboea. Site of a drawn battle between the Greek fleet and that of Xerxes (future king of Persia), in 480 BC.

Athena Greek goddess of war and wisdom, identified with the Roman Minerva. Daughter of Zeus and Metis, she was the tutelary patron of Athens.

Athenaeus (2ⁿᵈ or 3ʳᵈ century AD), Greek writer from Naucratis. Author of *The Sophists' Banquet*, a collection of curious anecdotes noted in the course of his reading.

Atoum Heliopolitan deity, represented as a king wearing a double crown. His sacred animals were the lion, the ichneumon (a kind of mongoose) and the snake.

Atum-Khepri another name for the sun god Ra. Khepri was the Egyptian name for the scarab (dung beetle), associated with the sun's regenerative powers.

Attica Greek peninsula, in ancient times the territory of Athens.

Augustus *Caius Julius Caesar Octavianus Augustus* (31 BC–14 AD), the first Roman emperor. Known as Octavian following his adoption by Caesar.

aule Greek word designating the residence of the court.

basileia Greek word signifying an area of buildings, including private residences, administrative buildings and military quarters, together with adjacent gardens.

Begram town in Afghanistan.

Bouto two towns in the Egyptian delta bear this name, which is associated with the idea of marshlands. One is situated on the Pelusiac arm of the Nile, south of Tanis; the other in the western delta, south of the marshes.

Bucephalus nickname signifying 'bullock's head' given to the uncontrollable horse which Alexander succeeded in taming, after recognising that it was afraid of its own shadow.

Busiris town in northern Egypt, the first to acknowledge Osiris as a god.

Byblos Phoenician city-state, present-day Jubail (in Lebanon), famous for its cult of Adonis.

Caepio (tower of) tower off Ebura, on the coast north of Gadeira (Cadiz).

Caesar *Gaius Julius Caesar* (100–44 BC), Roman general and statesman, and one of Cleopatra's lovers. He also wrote accounts of his military campaigns. In *The Alexandrian War*, written in Latin and almost certainly in fact the work of his lieutenant Hirtius, he records the events of the war of 48–47 BC.

Caligula Roman emperor who reigned from 37–41 AD. The mentally unbalanced son of Germanicus, he was famous for his cruelty and tyranny, and was finally assassinated.

Callimachus (c. 305–240 BC), Alexandrian poet and grammarian. Originally from Cyrene.

Callixenus of Rhodes Greek historian living c. 250 BC.

Campus Martius large wooded esplanade at Alexandria.

Canopos, Canobos name of the helmsman of Helen and Menelaus who is supposed to have given his name to the town of Canopus situated between Alexandria and the mouth of the western branch of the Nile.

Caracalla *Marcus Aurelius Antoninus Bassianus*, Roman emperor from 211–217 AD, known by the name of Caracalla. Responsible for the massacre of a large number of young Alexandrians.

casa del Fauno famous *villa* in Pompeii, housing a number of interesting artefacts (including a mosaic showing Alexander on his horse Bucephalus).

Chaeronea town in Boeotia, famous as the site of Philip II's victory over the Athenians and Thebans in 338 BC.

Chalcidice (Khalkidhikí) peninsula in northern Greece, ending in three promontories: Pallíni, Sithoniá and Aktí (where Mt Athos is located).

charis Greek word signifying 'that shines, that delights'. Rich in physical and moral connotations, it can be applied to such notions as beauty, kindness, grace, elegance, joy and pleasure.

chlamys short sleeveless tunic worn by riders, like those on the Parthenon frieze, and by *ephebes* ('beardless' or youth) undergoing military training.

chora name given to the countryside which supplied Greek towns with produce.

Cleopatra VII Queen of Egypt 51–30 BC, most famous of the Ptolemies.

Cnidus city in Caria, the original home of Sostratos, who built the lighthouse at Alexandria. The city was famous for its temple to Aphrodite and the statue of the goddess by Praxiteles.

Commodus Roman emperor who reigned from 180 to 193 AD. Son of Marcus Aurelius, the philosopher emperor.

crab bronze subfoundation of the Kaisarion obelisks. The Pharos lighthouse is said to have rested on similar structures.

Daphnae present-day Tell Defenneh, up-river from Pelusium. Fortress on the Pelusiac arm of the Nile.

Darius name belonging to several kings of Persia. The Darius whom Alexander defeated at the battle of Issos was Darius III Codoman.

Deinocrates of Rhodes architect who designed the lighthouse and the plan of Alexandria.

Demeter Greek goddess who had a sanctuary dedicated to her at Alexandria.

Denon (Dominique Vivant, Baron) (1747–1825), talented draughtsman and engraver, also a diplomat and administrator. He was Director of Museums under Napoleon I and responsible for setting up the Louvre.

Diades and Kharias engineers in the Macedonian army who advised Alexander regarding the layout of his city.

Diodorus Siculus (born c. 90 BC), Greek historian who visited Alexandria in 59 BC. In his *Bibliotheca historica*, he gives an account of the city's foundation and development.

Dio Cassius (155–235 AD), consul for the second time in 224. In his *History of Rome*, he describes the arrival of Octavian's fleet in the harbour at Alexandria and Antony's suicide in the mausoleum.

Douamoutef Egyptian god, son of Horus, represented with a dog's head.

Edku lake in the north-west of the Nile delta, now partially filled in.

Emesus town in Syria, on the Orontes. Famous for its temple dedicated to the Phoenician sun god Baal.

Emporium, Emporion market located alongside Alexandria's Portus Magnus. The word, signifying 'storehouse' or 'market', is used by Strabo to designate Alexandria's docks.

Epiphanus epithet signifying 'who manifests himself'.

Erinyes Greek goddesses of vengeance, known to the Romans as the Furies.

Eunostos Alexandria's western harbour, known as the 'port of safe return', whereas in reality it was dangerous and difficult to access.

Euphrates river in Asia, rising in Turkish Armenia and flowing through Syria into Iraq, where it joins the Tigris to form the Shatt al-Arab.

Euripides (480–406 BC), Greek dramatist, 18 of whose 92 tragedies survive.

Euxine Sea ancient name for the Black Sea, reputed for storms and hostile shore-dwellers.

Farouk I (1920–65), last king of Egypt, reigning from 1936 to 1952. He abdicated following a coup d'état.

Flavius Josephus (37–95 AD), Jewish historian, author of *The Jewish War*, in which he describes the harbour at Alexandria in precise detail.

Geb Egyptian god personifying the Earth, spouse of the sky goddess Nout.

Geta brother of Caracalla, who was assassinated by him in 212 AD.

Hades Greek god of the underworld, identified by the Romans as Pluto.

Halai administrative district of Attica between Marathon and Brauron, opposite the Petaliae islands. Present-day Rafina.

Heliopolis (from Greek *helios*, meaning 'sun') ancient city situated to the north of Cairo, dedicated to the cult of the sun god Ra.

Helios god of the sun in Greek mythology, counterpart to the Egyptian god Ra.

hellenica term that refers to objects or studies relating to ancient Greece.

Heptastadion artificial causeway linking the island of Pharos with the mainland.

Heracles Greek god known as Khonsu in ancient Egypt.

Hermanoubis Egyptian deity known as 'the great god who listens to us', an amalgam of Anubis, god of the dead, and Hermes, who served as a guide to the other world.

Hermes Greek god, known to the Romans as Mercury, recognisable by his winged sandals. Messenger of the gods and guide of travellers, he was also the protector of merchants, and of thieves.

Herodian (c. 175–250 AD), Roman historian, author of a *History of the Roman Emperors*. He highlights the importance of the city of Alexandria and describes the massacre by Caracalla.

Hippocrates Greek physician born in Kos *circa* 460 BC. He established a code of ethics which is the basis for the Hippocratic oath still sworn by doctors today. The *Hippocratic Collection* is a series of some 60 works recording his medical knowledge.

Hippodamus Greek architect from Miletus, a contemporary of Pericles. He invented the grid layout which was used at Alexandria.

Horemheb (1344–1314 BC), heir to an ancient family of the 18th nome (administrative division) of Upper Egypt. He fought against the Atonian heresy and usurped all the monuments dedicated to Tutankhamun.

Horus Egyptian solar deity usually depicted as a falcon or with a falcon's head. Son of Isis and Osiris, whose death he avenged by killing his murderer Set. His most famous statue is in the temple at Edfu.

hydrography mapping of the surface features of the sea-bed.

Ibn Battuta Arabic traveller and geographer who was born in Tangier in 1304 and died in Morocco between 1368 and 1377.

Isis Egyptian goddess, wife of Osiris and mother of the sun god Horus.

Jocasta wife of Oedipus, who slept with him without realising that he was her own son. Daughter of the Theban Menocenes and sister of Creon.

Julian Roman emperor who reigned from 361 to 363 AD. In his *Letters* he describes how the obelisk, carved at Heliopolis, was transported to Alexandria by Octavian in 12 BC and later shipped to Constantinople.

Kaisarion (also known as Cesarium and Sebasteion), one of Alexandria's most beautiful temples, built by Cleopatra VII in honour of Mark Antony.

Kebehsenouf Egyptian god, son of Horus, portrayed with a falcon's head.

Kibotos small artificial basin in Alexandria's western harbour, its box-like shape indicated by its name which translates as 'coffer'.

kom (plural *kiman*) earth mound.

Lagid name given to the Ptolemaic dynasty after its founder, Alexander's general, Lagos. It was originally thought that the name signified 'hare', but it actually means 'leader of people' (from *laos* and *agon*). The Lagid period lasted from 304 to 30 BC.

Leptis Magna town on the coast of Tripolitania (north-west Libya), also known as Neapolis, and having an excellent harbour.

Leucippe and Clitophon fictional work written in Greek by Achilles Tatius, in the 3rd century, celebrating the splendour of Alexandria.

Lochias (Cape) cape at Alexandria's eastern extremity, Cape Silsileh as it is known today.

Lucan (39–65 AD), Latin poet, author of the epic poem the *Pharsalia*, in which he describes Caesar's arrival by sea and entry into the city of Alexandria, the splendours of the palace and the siege of this building.

Lucian of Samosata (120–180 AD), Greek writer from the Syrian town of Samosata. Author of true stories, dialogues and satires.

Macedonia (kingdom of) central region of the Balkans, of great historical importance. The region is mountainous and has a number of basins, the waters from the largest of which (the Vardar Basin) flow into the Aegean. Philip II united the region's warlike tribes and was succeeded as king of Macedonia by his son Alexander the Great. Following Alexander's death, six Macedonian generals (the Diadochi) fought for control of his empire. The victory of Paulus Aemilius at Pydna, in 168 BC, put an end to Macedonian independence.

Maeander ancient name for the river Menderes in south-west Turkey.

Mareotis (Lake) present-day Lake Maryut, situated to the east of Alexandria.

Magnesia on the Maeander Thessalonian colony in Ionia.

Mahmoud Bey El-Falaky Egyptian astronomer who mapped ancient Alexandria in 1866.

Mahmoudieh (canal) freshwater canal bringing water to Alexandria from the Canopic arm of the Nile. Known for this reason as the 'good spirit' and represented as a tutelary serpent.

Maiandros garden in the city watered by a winding stream.

Mamelukes dynasty that sprang from a class of Turkish slave soldiers who seized power and ruled Egypt and Syria from 1250 to 1517.

Marathon village 40km north-east of Athens. Miltiades defeated the Persians there, and the exhausted runner Peidippides, charged with conveying the message of the Athenian victory, dropped dead on arrival in Athens.

Marcus Aurelius Roman emperor from 161 to 180 AD. His full title was *Imperator Caesar Marcus Aurelius Antoninus Augustus*. Caracalla, Roman emperor from 211 to 217, was anxious to adopt the name Marcus Aurelius, though his full title read *Imperator Caesar Marcus Aurelius Severus Antoninus Pius Aurelius*.

Medes a people of ancient Iran. The Median empire had its capital at Ecbatana and was overthrown by Cyrus the Great, King of Persia, c. 550 BC.

Megas Limin Greek name for Alexandria's Great Harbour or Portus Magnus.

Menelaus son of Atreus, King of Mycenae and brother of Agamemnon. He was married to Helen (whose abduction led to the Trojan War). Their daughter Hermione is frequently mentioned in the *Iliad* and the *Odyssey* as well as in the Greek tragedies.

Misenum promontory in Italy, on the western side of the Bay of Naples. Roman naval base.

Munichia harbour at Piraeus where the triremes were kept.

natron naturally occurring hydrated sodium carbonate, particularly plentiful in the delta (Wadi Natrun). It was used during the embalming process.

nemes Egyptian royal headdress.

Nephthys Egyptian goddess known for her role in the legend of Osiris. Sister of Isis, wife of Set and mother of Anubis.

nymphs female nature spirits, in Greek mythology, associated with woods, rivers and streams, and the sea.

Octavian name taken by Augustus after his adoption by Caesar.

Odyssey (The) epic poem, attributed like the *Iliad*, to Homer, recounting the adventures of Odysseus (Roman Ulysses) during his 10-year homeward wanderings after the fall of Troy.

Olympus small group of mountains in north-east Greece, on the border between Thessaly and Macedonia. Regarded by the ancient Greeks as the home of the gods.

Olynthus Greek city in Chalcidice on the north-west Aegean, destroyed by Philip of Macedonia in 348 BC.

Osiris-Apis Memphite god known in Alexandria as Serapis.

Osiris-Canopus image of Osiris, as he was worshipped at Canopus, in the form of a jug or vase surmounted by the god's head, also known as a Canopic vase.

Ounophris one of the names by which Osiris was known, meaning the 'Good Being' or the 'Kindly One'.

palation Greek word signifying 'the king's residence'.

Parthians a people related to the Scythians, who settled in the region south of the Caspian Sea (northeast Iran) in the 3rd century BC. Under Arsacius, Parthia expanded into a great empire dominating south-west Asia at the end of the 2nd century BC.

Pe-gouti Egyptian name for the city on the banks of the Nile which was named after Menelaus' helmsman, Canopos.

Pelusium sea port at Egypt's south-eastern limit. The city was known as 'the key to Egypt'.

Pericles (495–429 BC), Athenian statesman who presided over Athens' golden age.

pharaoh title of the ancient Egyptian kings, taken up by Greek sovereigns.

pharaonica name given by Prof. Jean Yoyotte to Alexandria's monuments, conceived in the time of the pharaohs and distinguishable from Hellenic culture in terms of type, style and hieroglyphic decoration.

Pharos small island off Alexandria which gave its name to the famous lighthouse. The name was originally applied to an imaginary island where, according to the Odyssey, Menelaus consulted the sea god Proteus.

Pharsalus town in Thessaly where Caesar defeated Pompey in 48 BC.

Philadelphus epithet signifying 'who loves his sister'.

philalexandrotatos epithet signifying 'a wholehearted friend of Alexander'.

Philip II of Macedonia (382–336 BC), regent in 359 and later King of Macedonia (356–336 BC), father of Alexander the Great. He defeated the joint forces of the Thebans and Athenians at the battle of Chaeronea in 338.

Philo of Alexandria (c. 11–50 AD), Greek writer who describes the borders of Lake Maerotis and the Alexandrian climate in his *De Vita Contemplativa*. In *In Flaccum*, he recounts Agrippa's journey from Pozzuoli to Alexandria.

Philoctetes legendary Greek hero who inherited from his father the bow and arrow of Heracles. On the way to Troy with the Greek expedition, he was abandoned on the island of Lemnos with a gangrenous wound contracted from a snake bite.

Plataea ancient city of Boeotia. In 479 BC, the allied Greek forces, led by Pausanias, inflicted a crushing defeat on the Persians at the battle of Plataea.

Plato (427–347 BC), Athenian philosopher, a devoted follower of Socrates.

Pliny the Elder (23–79 AD), Roman scholar, author of the *Natural History*, a universal encyclopedia written in Latin. He describes the site of Rhakotis and the fairways and obelisks in the Portus Magnus.

Plutarch (c. 46–120 AD), Greek moralist, philosopher and historian, author of the *Parallel Lives* (including biographies of Alexander, Julius Caesar and Mark Antony) and other works, providing valuable information on the history of Alexandria.

polis classical Greek term for a city and its territory.

Polybius (c. 202–120 BC), Greek historian who spent many years as a political hostage in Rome. He visited Alexandria in 140 BC and his *Histories* describe a number of Alexandrian monuments and street scenes.

Pompeii ancient city in Campania, in southern Italy, at the foot of Mount Vesuvius. It was buried under volcanic ash when Vesuvius erupted in 79 AD.

Pompey *Gnaeus Pompeius Magnus* (106–48 BC), Roman general and statesman. He formed the first Triumvirate with Crassus and Julius Caesar. Defeated by Caesar at Pharsalus in 48 BC, he fled to Egypt, where he was assassinated on the orders of Ptolemy XIII. His head was delivered to Caesar at Alexandria.

Porto Trajano port in Italy, on the Tyrrhenian Sea, opposite the island of Ilva.

Portus Magnus Latin name for Alexandria's eastern harbour. Separated from the Eustonos by the Heptastadion.

Poseidippos of Pella 3rd-century Greek poet who wrote a poem about the lighthouse.

Poseidon Greek god of the sea, in whose honour a sanctuary known as the Poseidium was built at Alexandria. Son of Cronus and Rhea, brother of Zeus and Hades.

Priene ancient city in Ionia, near Mount Mycale, at the mouth of the River Maeander.

Procopius of Gaza principal Byzantine historian at the time of Justinian I. He wrote about Caesarea and Palestine at the beginning of th 6th century AD.

Prometheus son of the Titan Japet and 'cousin' of Zeus. He is said to have fashioned humans from clay and to have stolen fire – to give to man – from Hephaestus' forge on Mount Olympus. As punishment, Zeus chained him to a rock in the Caucasus and sent an eagle to devour his liver (which grew back each night).

Proteus god of the sea, in the *Odyssey*, whose job was to shepherd the herds of seals and other sea creatures. He had a hideaway on the island of Pharos.

Pseudo-Callisthenes (2nd or 3rd century AD), author of the *Story of Alexander*, in which he describes the foundation of the city of Alexandria and its monuments.

Ptah Egyptian creator god, a local deity of Memphis, depicted in human form, tightly bound in long mummy wrappings. The Greeks identified him with Hephaestus.

Puteoli port in Italy, on the Gulf of Naples. Present-day Pozzuoli.

Qait-Bey 15th-century Mameluke ruler who built the fort protecting the roads at Alexandria.

Quintus Curtius (living during the reign of Claudius, 41–54 AD), author of *Histories*, in which he refers to the foundation of Alexandria.

Ra, Re, Egyptian sun god, usually portrayed with a falcon's head surmounted by a solar disc and serpent.

Raya de Behera Canal constructed in 1860, linking Khatatbeh with the delta.

regia Latin equivalent of Greek *basileia*.

Salamis island off the west coast of Attica.

Septimius Severus *Lucius Septimius Severus Pertinax*, Roman emperor who reigned from 193 to 211 AD. He was helped to power by the Illyrian legions, took Mesopotamia from the Parthians and fortified the northern frontier of Britain.

Serapis principal deity of Alexandria, where he had a temple (there was also one in Canopus).

Set Egyptian deity identified with Typhon by the Greeks. Originally a sun and sky god, he murdered his brother Osiris and so came to represent all evil. His sacred animals were the pig, donkey, hippopotamus and desert oryx. He is portrayed in a peculiar composite form, with the body of a greyhound, a long, straight, forked tail, slender muzzle and long ears.

Seven Wonders of the World the supreme man-made structures of the ancient world: the Great Pyramid at Giza in Egypt, the Hanging Gardens of Babylon, the statue of Zeus at Olympia, the temple of Artemis at Ephesus, the Mausoleum of Halicarnassus, the Colossus of Rhodes and the Lighthouse of Alexandria.

Sieglin (Ernst von) archaeologist closely involved in explorations at Alexandria, who excavated, amongst other things, the necropolis of Kômesch-Schukâfa.

Silsileh (Cape) current name of Cape Lochias.

Sophilos artist who signed the mosaic found at Thmouis representing the city of Alexandria as a woman wearing a ship's prow on her head.

Sophocles (495–405 BC), Greek dramatist, seven of his 105 tragedies are extant.

Sosibios guardian of the young Ptolemy V Epiphanes.

Sostratos of Cnidus distinguished architect and engineer, son of Dexiphanes of Cnidus. According to an epigram attributed to the poet Poseidippos, he was responsible for constructing the lighthouse at Alexandria.

Strabo (66 BC–24 AD), Greek geographer from Amaseia (now Amasya, Turkey), who travelled in Egypt and visited Alexandria between 27 and 20 BC, where the prefect of Egypt acted as his host and guide. He wrote a *Geography*, in which he discusses Alexandria and describes the city in detail.

taenia narrow strip of land bordering the Egyptian coastline. It was also the name given to a single line of poetry.

Theocritus (310–250 BC), Greek poet living during the reign of Ptolemy II Philadelphus. He wrote a series of *Idylls*, two of which (XV and XVII) are brief tableaux of life in Alexandria.

Thmouis town to the east of the Egyptian delta, in the nome of Mendes.

Thoth (Greek Hermes), Egyptian moon deity, depicted with the head of an ibis and particularly venerated at Hermopolis. His sphere of influence encompassed all areas of intellectual thought, including writing, language and the calendar.

Thrace (Sea of) stretch of water lying southeast of Europe and northeast of Greece.

Timon of Athens disillusioned sage, famous for his sarcasm and sardonic wit. He lived at the time of the Peloponnesian War (431–404 BC).

Timonium private residence (which has now disappeared) named after the misanthrope Timon, in Alexandria's eastern harbour. It was here that Mark Antony planned to retreat from the world.

Tlepolemos officer under Ptolemy IV Philopator who inspired the revolt against Agathocles.

Tritons helpers of Poseidon, god of the sea.

troglodytes cave dwellers in Ethiopia and along the shores of the Red Sea.

Tubi Egyptian month roughly corresponding to our month of January.

Zeus supreme deity in Greek mythology, god of light and thunder and ruler of the heavens.

Bibliography

Bernand A., 'Les confins libyques', *Mémoires de l'Institut français d'archéologie orientale du Caire*, XCI, 1970.

Bernand A., 'Sur le marbre du phare d'Alexandrie', *Zeitschrift für Papyrologie und Epigraphik*, 118, 1997.

Bernand A. and Bernand E., 'L'épigraphie sous-marine dans le port oriental d'Alexandrie', *Zeitschrift für Papyrologie und Epigraphik*, 121, 1998.

Canfora L., *la Véritable Histoire de la bibliothèque d'Alexandrie*, Éditions Desjonquéres, Paris, 1988.

Chamoux F., 'Hommages à Claire Préaux', *Chronique d'Égypte*, Brussels, 1976.

El-Abadi M., *Vie et destin de l'ancienne bibliothèque d'Alexandrie*, Ateliers de l'Unesco, Paris, 1990.

Goddio F., *À la recherche de Cléopâtre*, Éditions Robert Laffont, Paris, 1996.

Goddio F. et al., *Alexandria: the submerged royal quarters*, Periplus Publishing London Ltd, London, 1998.

Hesse A. et al., 'L'Heptastade d'Alexandrie', *Études Alexandrines 6 : Alexandrina 2*, Empereur J.-Y. (ed.), IFAO, le Caire, 2002.

Yoyotte J., 'Les vraies questions sur Alexandrie', *L'Histoire*, 229, 1999.

Yoyotte J. and Charvet P., *Strabon : Le voyage en Égypte*, Éditions NiL, Paris, 1997.

Chronology

This table situates in time the noteworthy people, events of Alexandrine history and circumstances known through literary tradition which contributed to the destruction of the city's monuments and the innundation of its shores. It should not be forgotten that often this destruction took place in circumstances not reported by the ancient texts, especially the circumstances of the flooding, which may have been the result of numerous landslides and subsidence.

Pharaohs, whose monuments have been rediscovered in Alexandria

XIIth **Dynasty**	
Sesostris I	1971–1926 BC
Sesostris II	1897–1878
Sesostris III	1878–1843
XVIIIth **Dynasty**	
Tuthmosis III	1478–1426
Tuthmosis IV	1401–1391
Amenhotep III	1391–1353
Horemheb	1323–1293
XIXth **Dynasty**	
Seti I	1291–1279
Rameses II	1279–1213
Merenptah	1213–1204
Seti II	1204–1192
XXth **Dynasty**	
Rameses IX	1120–1103
XXVIth **Dynasty (Saitic)**	
Psamtik I	664–610
Nekau	610–595
Psamtik II	595–589
Apries	589–570
Ahmose	570–526
XXVIIth **Dynasty (Persian)**	525–404
XXVIIIth **Dynasty (Saitic)**	404–399
XXIXth **Dynasty (Mendesian)**	
Hakoris	393–380
XXXth **Dynasty (Sebennytic)**	
Nekhtnebef (Nectanebo I)	380–363
Nekhthorhebe (Nectanebo II)	360–343
Second Persian Period	343–332

Hellenistic Era

Alexander the Great in Egypt	332
Lagid Dynasty	
Ptolemy I Soter	305–283
Ptolemy II Philadelphus	285–246
Ptolemy III Euergetes	246–221
Ptolemy IV Philopator	221–204
Ptolemy V Epiphanes	204–180
Ptolemy VI Philometor	180–145
Ptolemy VIII Euergetes II	145–116
Ptolemy IX Soter II Lathyrus	116–80
Ptolemy X Alexander I	110–88
Ptolemy XI Alexander II	80
Ptolemy XII Auletes	80–51
Cleopatra VII	51–30
with Ptolemy XIII	52–47
with Ptolemy XIV	47–44
with Ptolemy XV Caesar	43–30
Julius Caesar in Egypt	48–46
Mark Antony in Egypt	41–30
Octavian in Alexandria	30

Roman Era

Augustus (=Octavian Caesar)	28 BC–14 AD
Tiberius	14–37
Caius Caligula	37–41
Claudius	41–54
Nero	54–68
Domitian	81–96
Trajan	98–117
Hadrian	117–138
Commodus	180–192
Septimius Severus	193–211
Caracalla	211–217
Diocletian	284–305

Christianisation

Conversion of Constantine the Great	324–332
Constantius II	337–361
Destruction of the Mithraeum	360
Julian the Apostate	361–363
Valens	364–378
Tidal wave at Alexandria	365
Theodosius the Great	379–395
Destruction of the Serapeum by Bishop Theophilus	391
Continued elimination of pagan temples and building of churches	c. 360–414
Closing of the temple of Isis at Menouthis	c. 485

Arab-islamic Era

Capture of Alexandria by Amr Ibn el-As	641
The first Caliphs	641–661
The Omayyad Caliphs	661–750
The Abbasid Caliphs	750–969
Earthquake at Alexandria	796
The Tulunids	850–905
Earthquake at Alexandria and as far as Fustât	950, 959
The Fatimid Caliphs	969–1171
The Ayyubid Sultans	1174–1250
Saladin	1174–1195
The Mamelukes	1251–1517
Earthquakes at Alexandria and as far as Upper Egypt	1258, 1268
Baibars	1294–1310
Earthquake at Alexandria and in the whole of Egypt, and repairs	1303–1304
Earthquake at Alexandria	1341
Qait-Bey	1468–1496
Conquest of Egypt by the Ottoman Empire	
Selim I	1517

Acknowledgements

The missions in the Portus Magnus were undertaken with the support of the Hilti Foundation, without which the important cartographical and archaeological discoveries made since 1996 would not have been possible.

Franck Goddio would like to thank:
Farouk Hosni, Egyptian Minister for Culture;
Prof. Zahi Hawass, Secretary General of the Egyptian Supreme Council for Antiquities;
Mohamed Abdel Salam Al Mahgoub, Governor of Alexandria;
Gilles Gauthier, French Consul General in Alexandria;
The Elf Foundation for its support of the first electronic prospection mission undertaken in 1992;
Ahmed Abdel Fattah, Director of Museums and Archaeological Sites in Alexandria;
Prof. Gaballah Ali Gaballah;
Ibrahim A. Darwish and all the members of the Department of Underwater Archaeology of the Egyptian Supreme Council for Antiquities;
Amira Abou Bakr;
Doria Saïd;
and Sophie Lalbat.

Periplus Publishing London Ltd would like to thank, in particular, Jean Yoyotte, Professeur honoraire au Collège de France, for proofreading the manuscript, as well as giving precious advice, additions and corrections.

We would also like to thank:
Étienne Bernand, Professeur honoraire des Universités;
Prof. Françoise Dunand of the University of Strasbourg,
Arthur de Graauw, marine engineer at SOGREAH Engineering, Grenoble;
and Prof. Zsolt Kiss of the Centre for Mediterranean Archaeology of the Warsaw Academy of Sciences;
whose texts published in the book *Alexandria: the submerged royal quarters* (Periplus Publishing London Ltd, London, 1998), were used as a source for the results of the excavations undertaken by Franck Goddio and his team.

Picture credits

Jérôme Delafosse © Franck Goddio / HILTI Foundation
8, 13 (bottom), 14, 15, 22 (bottom), 34 (top), 34 (bottom), 34 (middle), 35 (top), 35 (bottom), 36, 44 (top), 44 (bottom), 45 (bottom), 46, 52 (middle right), 53 (top), 53 (bottom), 54 (top), 55, 56 (top), 56 (middle), 65 (top), 76, 78 (bottom), 79, 81, 82–3, 85 (right), 90, 91 (all images), 95, 96 (bottom), 98–9, 100, 101 (top), 126 (top), 127, 128 (top), 135, 136–7.

Christoph Gerigk © Franck Goddio / HILTI Foundation
4 (top), 4 (bottom), 13 (top), 16 (top), 16 (bottom), 17, 24 (portrait), 28–9, 30 (top), 30 (middle), 30 (bottom), 32 (portrait), 33 (bottom), 37 (top), 37 (bottom), 38, 39 (top), 39 (bottom), 40–1, 42 (portrait), 45 (top), 48 (portrait), 50–1, 52 (portrait), 52 (top left), 52 (middle left), 52 (bottom left), 52 (top right), 52 (bottom right), 54 (bottom), 60 (bottom), 61 (top), 61 (middle), 61 (bottom), 62–3, 64 (portrait), 64 (bottom), 65 (middle), 65 (bottom), 68–9, 80, 96 (top), 97, 101 (bottom), 103, 104 (bottom), 105, 110–11, 113 (top), 115, 116, 117 (top), 118 (bottom), 119, 122 (bottom), 124 (top), 126 (bottom), 150–1, 176.

Frédéric Osada © Franck Goddio / HILTI Foundation
3, 22 (top), 22 (middle), 31, 32 (bottom), 78 (top), 88 (top), 94, 104 (top), 113 (bottom), 118 (top), 120, 121, 122 (top), 123, 125 (bottom), 132 (top), 133 (top), 134 (top).

Fernando Pereira © Franck Goddio / HILTI Foundation
56 (bottom), 57 (all images), 58–9 (all images), 72, 73, 74, 75, 88 (bottom), 128 (bottom), 129 (top), 140 (top), 140 (bottom), 141 (top), 141 (bottom), 145 (top), 145 (bottom), 156, 158, 159 (top), 159 (bottom), 160, 161, 162 (top), 162 (bottom), 163, 164–5.

Samia Hamidi
60 (portrait).

Franck Goddio / HILTI Foundation
24, 26, 27, 43, 49, 66, 67 (top), 77, 89 (top), 89 (bottom), 112 (bottom), 124 (bottom), 125 (top), 129 (bottom), 131, 132 (bottom), 133 (bottom), 134 (bottom), 144, 147, 149, 157 (top), 157 (bottom).

Periplus
33 (top), 42 (bottom), 43 (top).

The American Numismatic Society
84 (top), 84 (bottom), 85 (left), 85 (middle), 107 (top).

RMN
106 Gérard Blot, Châteaux de Malmaison et Bois Préau;
107 (bottom) Lagiewski, musée des Beaux-Arts, Lyon; 108 C. Jean, Louvre;
109 Michèle Bellot, Louvre D.A.G.